African American Leaders

of Maryland

African American Leaders

of Maryland

A PORTRAIT GALLERY

Suzanne Ellery Chapelle

&

Glenn O. Phillips

Baltimore

MARYLAND HISTORICAL SOCIETY

Library of Congress Cataloging-in-Publication Data

Chapelle, Suzanne Ellery Greene.
    African American leaders of Maryland: a portrait gallery /
Suzanne Ellery Chapelle, Glenn O. Phillips.
       p. cm.
    Includes bibliographical references (p.) and index.
    ISBN 0-938420-69-0 (alk. paper)
       1. African Americans—Maryland—Biography. 2. African
    Americans—Maryland—Portraits. 3. African Americans—Maryland—
    History. 4. African American leadership—Maryland—History.
    5. Maryland—Biography. I. Phillips, Glenn O. II. Title.

    E185.93.M2 C48 2002
    920'.009296073—dc21
    [B]
                                                                    2002071842

Manufactured in China.
The paper used in this publication meets the minimum requirements of the
American National Standard for Information Sciences Permanence of Paper for
Printed Library Materials ANSI Z39.48-1984

Contents

THROUGH THE CENTURIES

THE PORTRAIT GALLERY

Chronology

Benjamin Banneker (1731–1806) — Scientist and Surveyor

Daniel Isaac Wright Coker (1780–1846) — Minister and Teacher

Mary Elizabeth Lange (1784–1882) — Religious Leader and Educator

Josiah Henson (1789–1883) — Abolitionist and Businessman

James W. C. Pennington (1807–1870) — Clergyman, Writer, Abolitionist

Daniel Bashiel Warner (1815–1880) — President, Republic of Liberia

Henry Highland Garnet (1815–1882) — Clergyman and Abolitionist

Samuel Ringgold Ward (1817–1866) — Abolitionist

Frederick Douglass (c. 1818–1895) — Abolitionist and Statesman

Harriet Tubman (c. 1821–1913) — Abolitionist

Frances Ellen Watkins Harper (1825–1911) — Poet and Lecturer

Isaac Myers (1835–1891) — Labor Leader and Businessman

Ann Maria Weems (1840–unknown) — Abolitionist

Christian Abraham Fleetwood (1840–1914) — Civil War Soldier and Civil Servant

John Henry Murphy, Sr. (1840–1922) — Journalist and Businessman

William Henry Bishop (1849–1904) — Physician and Activist

John Edward Bruce (1856–1924) — Journalist

Augustus Walley (1856–1938) — Buffalo Soldier and Army Officer

George Freeman Bragg, Jr. (1863–1940) — Episcopal Clergyman and Author

Harry Sythe Cummings (1866–1917) — Politician, Lawyer, Businessman

Matthew Henson (1866–1955) — Explorer

Ida Rebecca Cummings (1867–1958) — Teacher and Volunteer

Joseph "Baby" Joe Gans (1874–1910) — Boxing Champion

George "Father Divine" Baker (1879–1965) — Religious Leader

John Thomas Quander (1880–1910) — Physician

James Hubert "Eubie" Blake (1883–1983) — Jazz Composer and Musician

Carl John Murphy (1889–1967) — Publisher and Activist

Lillie Carroll Jackson (1889–1975) — Community Leader

Edward Franklin Frazier (1894–1962) — Sociologist

Albert Irvin Cassell (1895–1969) — Architectural Engineer

Benjamin Arthur Quarles (1904–1996) — Historian

James Amos Porter (1905–1970) — Artist and Art Historian

Verda Freeman Welcome (1907–1990) — State Senator

Cabell Calloway III (1907–1994) — Musician and Composer

Thurgood Marshall (1908–1993) — Supreme Court Justice

Pauli Murray (1910–1985) — Lawyer, Professor, Priest

Vivien T. Thomas (1910–1985) — Surgical Technician and Researcher

N. Louise Young (1910–1997)	Physician
Clarence Maurice Mitchell, Jr. (1911–1984)	Journalist, Lawyer, Lobbyist
Billie Eleanora Holiday (1915–1959)	Jazz Singer
Leon Day (1916–1995)	Baseball Player
Silas Edwin Craft (1918–1995)	Educator and Activist
Phyllis Ann Wallace (1921–1993)	Economist
Harry Augustus Cole (1921–1999)	Attorney and Judge
Reginald Francis Lewis (1942–1993)	Businessman and Philanthropist

Preface

Maryland has over the centuries produced within its African American community a striking cluster of spontaneously energetic and creative personalities. Despite the state's modest land mass and population size, an extraordinary number of African American leaders have been born in or lived in Maryland. Many are among the best-known names in any examination of American history, ranging from Benjamin Banneker to Harriet Tubman and Frederick Douglass to Reginald Lewis. Nevertheless, there are other Marylanders of African descent who have lived extraordinary lives and accomplished fascinating feats whose tales are equally stirring and inspiring and need to be told.

Our initial interest in working on this project was stimulated by Robert I. Cottom, who had the strong conviction that a collection of Maryland's African American biographies would bring a new perspective to and deeper appreciation for the history of Maryland's pivotal role in producing a more just society in America.

This work intends to provide readers with information about some of the most extraordinary Marylanders. It illustrates how under the many, varied, and difficult circumstances they encountered in Maryland, from indentured life and slavery to racial segregation, these individuals and many others overcame tremendous obstacles. Furthermore, these individuals were often able to improve the quality of life for others and thus have positively influenced the wider community. Above all, we desire to show the limitless possibilities of the human spirit. We have also included an overview that narrates the principal issues, challenges, and personalities that have made the life of African Americans in this state so intriguing.

Collective biographies of African Americans have existed for many years, an early example being William Wells Brown's *The Black Man: His Antecedents, His Genius, and His Achievements* (1863). However, there have been fewer collections of biographies that have concentrated on personalities from a single state. George F. Bragg's 1925 publication, *Men of Maryland,* was probably the first attempt to assemble short biographies of Maryland's African American achievers. We have examined the latest research completed on our subjects and included some of the findings in this narrative.

The task of this work is to assemble and capture the origins, trials, and triumphs of forty-five of Maryland's most fascinating individuals of African descent. Many of them helped to shape lives in their community, the state of Maryland, the rest of the country and, in many cases, around the world. Our selection process attempted to include a wide variety of persons from all walks of life, from the eighteenth to the twentieth centuries. Persons still living at the end of the twentieth century were not considered for inclusion. While having a Maryland birthplace was important in the selection process, it was not the defining criterion. Consequently, there are a few included who were not born in Maryland but who spent much of their lives in the state and whose activities have had a profound influence on Maryland's—or the nation's—history. It is equally interesting to note that a significant percentage who were born in Maryland lived most of their lives outside of Maryland and rose to prominence in other parts of our nation. Clearly this collection of biographies is not intended to be the definitive list of outstanding Marylanders of African ancestry. Rather, it should be viewed as a selection of important individuals whose lives reflect what life in Maryland has represented over the centuries.

It is our hope that readers will be inspired by the highlights offered on the lives of these outstanding Marylanders to pursue further and more in-depth readings about these individuals beginning with the recommended readings included at the end of the book. There were many other highly deserving and accomplished Marylanders who were not included. Among these are eighteenth-century Marylander Joshua Johnson, the well-known early-American portrait painter, the courageous nineteenth-century abolitionist Hezekiah Grice, and dozens of others. Our inability to locate clearly verifiable portraits of these persons at this time prevented their biographies from being included, as this was one major criterion for inclusion in the portrait gallery. Nevertheless, the lives of the men and women in this portrait gallery vividly remind us of our rich past, a past that until recent decades has been ignored but that should make us all proud of our human triumphs in Maryland.

In a project such as this, one becomes indebted to people who have contributed to the book in a variety of ways. We would like to acknowledge our many helpers and thank them for advice, photos, information, and support. Especially we would like to thank Dr. Robert I. Cottom of the Press at the Maryland Historical Society for his interest in adding to the written history of African Americans in Maryland, for his commitment to this book, and for his hard work and expertise. We also would like to give great thanks to editors Donna Shear and Patricia Anderson for their encouragement and their unstinting labor on the many tasks that made this book more than just an idea.

We deeply appreciate the contributions of many colleagues at Morgan State University, especially Dr. Burney J. Hollis, dean of the College of Liberal Arts, and Dr. Annette Palmer, chairperson of the Department of History, for release time that helped make completion of this project possible. We thank Patricia Thomas for typing essay drafts and also Charlotte Stewart, Dr. Ruhul Amin, and Dr. Raymond Winbush, all of the Urban Institute for their support. We deeply appreciate the help of Dr. Donna Tyler Hollie who generously shared her knowledge of the African American community in Baltimore. Special thanks go to friends and colleagues Barbara Lamb and Jack Goellner for advice on the ins and outs of the publishing process and to Dr. Jean Russo, an expert on Maryland colonial history and on the history of Annapolis, who generously shared her considerable expertise.

Librarians are the experts on locating information, and we are indebted to many for their assistance as we researched our subjects. The wonderful staff members of the African American and Maryland Collections at the Enoch Pratt Free Library, Vivian Fisher, Jeff Korman, and Eva Slezak, expertly searched for resources through the years. Morgan State University reference librarians Maggie Wanza, James Yuan, Donald Matthews, and Charles Mezu assisted in locating some rare publications and other sources. The most difficult part of a book like this one is obtaining high-quality photographs. In fact, we had to leave out several biographies we wanted to include because of the lack of availability of such photos. Our list of thanks to archivists, family members and other individuals for helping us locate these photos is long. We thank Clinton Coleman and Frederick Douglass IV of the Morgan State University Office of Public Relations; Rob Schoeberlein, Emily Oland Squires, and Emily Murphy of the Maryland State Archives; and Dave Prencipe, Ruth Mitchell, and Mary Markey of the Maryland Historical Society. We thank Mrs. Vivien Thomas, Rohulamin Quander, the Scurlock family, Mrs. Dorothye Craft, Mrs. Loida M. N. Lewis, the late Ambassador Nathaniel Gibson, and the family of Harry Sythe Cummings for photographs of friends and family members and images from their private collections. We further thank archivists and librarians whose knowledge of their collections helped us procure the best available photos: Bill Burdick of the National Baseball Hall of Fame and Museum; Greg Schwalenberg of the Babe Ruth Museum; Pamela Stuedemann of the Art Institute of Chicago; Beth Howse, special collections librarian at Fisk University; Marie-Helene Gold at the Arthur and Elizabeth Schlesinger Library on the History of American Women at Radcliffe College; Marjorie Winslow Kehoe at the Alan Mason Chesney Archives of the Johns Hopkins Medical Institutions; Bruce Scherer of the Historical Society of Pennsylvania; Jenny O'Neil of the Massachusetts Institute of Technology Museum; Christine Mosser, special collections librarian at the Toronto Reference Library; Father John Bowen of the Sulpician Archives in Baltimore; Dr. Cliff Muse, archivist, and Donna Wells, head of photographs and prints at the Manuscript Division of the Moorland Spingarn Research Center at Howard University; Mary Yearwood of the Arthur Schomburg Center for Research; Donald Bowden of AP/World Wide Photos of New York; and the staff at the Library of Congress and the Martin Luther King Library in Washington, D.C.

Finally, and most important, we thank our families who have lived with this book and continued to encourage us for the several years it took to finish. Glenn thanks his wife Ingrid and daughter Mariette of Silver Spring, Maryland and his brother Dion of the University of the Virgin Islands in St. Thomas, for the great blessing of their loving support. Sue thanks her daughter Jenny for love, joy, support, patience, and friendship through this and many other endeavors.

Suzanne Ellery Greene Chapelle
Glenn O. Phillips
Baltimore, Maryland
September 2003

Through the Centuries . . .

African Americans in Maryland

A
FRICAN AMERICANS HAVE BEEN INTEGRAL to Maryland's history since the earliest colonial times. This brief essay provides an overview of the history of African Americans in Maryland and also the local and national context in which their experiences took place. Specific individuals and families are highlighted to give the course of history a human face. Many of these stories also suggest further research waiting to be undertaken. This narrative provides the background needed to understand the achievements of and challenges to the men and women whose biographies follow.

The Seventeenth Century

Records show that there were two men of African descent among the first group of settlers in colonial Maryland. We have information about only one of them, Mathias de Sousa. In November 1633 two sailing ships, the *Ark* and the *Dove*, left England and sailed past the Canary Islands, the Cape Verde Islands, and Barbados and St. Kitts in the West Indies. Finally, in early 1634, the small ships sailed up the Potomac River and arrived at what is now St. Mary's County in southern Maryland. On board was Mathias de Sousa, a man of African descent, an indentured servant of a Jesuit priest, Father Andrew White, who had come to minister to the spiritual needs of this new colony. The colony's proprietor or owner was Cecilius Calvert, an English Roman Catholic, who held the title Lord Baltimore and was denied full citizenship in his homeland because of his religion. Mathias de Sousa served out the term of his indenture and became free. Like other freemen of the colony, he could vote in person in the General Assembly. He worked for a while as captain of a ship that engaged in trade with local American Indians. Mathias de Sousa was the first of many men and women of African ancestry who made an important contribution to Maryland's history.[1]

The earliest Africans in Maryland were not slaves for life but rather had an ambiguous legal status that included indentured servitude for a limited number of years. Many European workers also served under this contractual arrangement. At the end of a specified number of years, indentured servants became free, were able to own land, to testify in court and, if they were male and owned the requisite amount of property, had the right to vote. Records from the seventeenth century contain a number of cases in which blacks such as John Babtiste, Thomas Hagleton, and Ralph Trunkett successfully sued in court for their freedom based on a contract for a specific number of years of service.[2] Records from Somerset County (which then included present-day Wicomico and Worcester Counties) have preserved the story of Anthony and Mary Johnson and their sons, John and Richard Johnson. This free black family moved from the Eastern Shore of Virginia to Somerset County in the mid-1660s. In 1666, Anthony and John leased a 300-acre lot and in 1670 recorded their livestock brand in the county courthouse. In 1677, John bought a forty-four-acre farm that he named Angola. The last surviving record of Angola comes from 1706 when John's son, John, died without an heir and the land reverted to the proprietor of the colony.[3]

As settlers moved up the Western Shore of the Chesapeake, Africans as well as white indentured servants also became free landowners after their arrival. One of these families, that of a slave named Bannaka and his wife Molly, later gained national prominence. Around 1683 an English woman named Molly Welsh, who had chosen indentured servitude over a possible death sentence for stealing (in reality, spilling) some milk on the farm where she worked, arrived in Baltimore County where she worked out the term of her indenture. She eventually bought land and two male African slaves to help her farm the property. She freed both men, perhaps because she herself knew what it was like to be unfree. Bannaka, who had been born in Senegal and was probably of Wolof origin, and Molly married. They had a daughter named Mary, born free, who married an African-born man named Robert. Robert had been captured, probably in the 1720s, and enslaved in "Guinea," the name given to the whole West Coast of Africa from present-day Ghana to Nigeria. Robert was so rebellious and escaped so many times that he was finally freed. When Robert and Mary married, he assumed her last name, then rendered Bannekey. Mary and Robert were the parents of Benjamin Banneker.[4] Free families such as the Johnsons and the Bannekers are a part of Maryland's early colonial history that warrants further study.

During these same early decades, the system that so cruelly enslaved many men, women, and children was developed. Thirteen Africans were brought to St. Mary's City for sale in 1642. Others followed. As more Africans were brought to the colony, stricter controls were put into practice. The earliest comprehensive slave law, passed by the Maryland Assembly in 1663, stated that all blacks brought into the colony would be presumed to be slaves for life, unless they could prove that they had a contract. It further required that their children would be slaves for life. Because Christianity was often cited by judges as a reason for granting freedom to an African petitioner, Maryland passed a law in 1664 that decreed that baptism should not affect the legal status of a slave. Early laws also tried to limit marriages between blacks and whites, which clearly took place frequently enough that opponents of such interracial mixing worked hard to discourage it. One such law required that a white woman who bore the child of a male slave would herself be enslaved and that the child would also be a slave.

Slave Quarters, St. Mary's County, Md. Maryland Historical Society.

Until 1690 relatively few Africans lived in Maryland. White servants performed most of the manual labor. The colony was sparsely settled and much of it was covered with forests. Most people, except Native Americans, lived on farms built along the banks of rivers. Boats provided the most efficient transportation. In the last decade of the seventeenth century, the colony's economy began to change. Tobacco, the most profitable crop in both Maryland and Virginia, was bringing a high price in Europe, and landowners wanted to invest their profits. More land and more workers, both black and white, meant still greater profits for the landowners. As a small percentage of the colonists became wealthy, they were eager for slave labor to do the work of producing the tobacco crop, which was the cornerstone of the colony's financial success. After 1690, the supply of European workers declined, and Maryland's elite increasingly relied on African slaves to do the work. In 1697, there were around 3,000 slaves in Maryland. By 1710, the number had risen to nearly 8,000, about 18 percent of the colony's total population. By 1755, when a census was taken in Maryland, approximately 45,000 residents were of African descent. This was 30 percent of the colony's total population. Of that number, 28 percent were either born in Africa or were of African ancestry and 2 percent were of mixed African and European ancestry.[5] Native Americans were not counted, nor were people of mixed African and Native American parentage who lived among the Indians.

The first generation of slaves endured the horrors of the Middle Passage aboard ships where human beings were crowded into holds, chained, allowed only small amounts of disgustingly unsanitary water and food, and forced to live in filth. Many died. Some chose suicide. Others became sick and arrived in America weak, starved, and terrified. Some, like Benjamin Banneker's father, remained rebellious. Most Africans brought to Maryland came from West Africa, many from the area that is now Nigeria. "Kunta Kinte," according to Alex Haley, arrived in 1767 in Annapolis aboard the *Lortt Ligonier,* which had sailed from the Gambia River.[6] Some slaves were brought from Caribbean islands such as Barbados for sale in Maryland. Over time, an increasing number of both slaves and free blacks were native-born.

Many slaves lived in the southern Maryland tobacco-growing counties of Anne Arundel, Calvert, Charles, Prince George's and St. Mary's. Their work was the basis of the wealth that made a few large landowners very rich and powerful. In the major tobacco-producing areas, between 40 and 50 percent of the population was black. Most men and women worked long hours in the fields planting, tending, and harvesting crops. Children from around the age of seven were required to join the grown-ups in the fields. They could pick up stones or pick insects from the plants. Only very young children, under the care of elderly women, did not join in that work. In the Eastern Shore counties of Dorchester, Kent, Queen Anne's, and Talbot, slaves and free blacks grew tobacco, worked in more diversified agriculture, and also worked in towns. Northern Maryland had the smallest percentage of slaves, but even there African Americans contributed to the economy in important ways.

Throughout the colony, some slaves learned skilled crafts such as carpentry and blacksmithing. Others worked at household jobs including child care, cooking, cleaning, and taking care of the always important stables. Both slaves and free men worked in the shipbuilding industry that grew in towns along Maryland's many waterways. African Americans labored in colonial ironworks such as the one at Principio Creek in Cecil County and the Baltimore Iron Works. As wheat became the most important crop in central and western Maryland, demand for slaves declined in those areas. Tobacco needed a lot of tending, but wheat required intense labor only at harvest time. Furthermore, especially in the western part of the colony, many landowners had small farms and either could not afford slaves or disapproved of slavery. German families immigrating from neighboring Pennsylvania and other small farmers usually did the work themselves, perhaps with the help of a few hired hands during the harvest season.[7]

Slave family life varied greatly. During the first generation, there were many more men than women. Male workers were in the highest demand and brought the highest prices in the slave markets. To prevent plots of rebellion or escape, owners often deliberately put together people who spoke different languages. Life was not only brutal but often lonely. With the second generation and the natural birth ratio, the numbers of males and females became more even, and English became the common language. On large plantations, with large slave communities, some families managed to stay intact. Generally, young children were kept with their mothers. Husbands and older children were frequently sold. Often, but not always, they did remain in the vicinity, so family visits were possible during the evening and on Sundays. Extended family networks developed and remained an important part of community life. On large plantations slaves generally lived together in the "quarters," which allowed some privacy and the opportunity to maintain some of their African cultural heritage. When a less wealthy owner had only one or two slaves, those slaves generally slept in the same house as the owner or in the loft of a barn. They had few opportunities to socialize with other blacks and generally were more isolated.

Throughout the slave period in Maryland, men and women protested frequently in a variety of ways. Many ran away from their masters' properties. Some joined Native Americans in forests or wetland areas. Others rebelled. In 1739–40, one courageous African American born in Prince George's County, Jack Ransom, led a number of slaves, many said to be African-born, in an uprising. They planned to kill their masters in order to obtain their freedom. The plot was discovered, and Ransom was tried and hanged for his leading role.[8] Passive protests were more common and still could result in harsh punishments. Not only the physical brutality and the breaking up of families but also the utter lack of ability to control one's own fate often led people to despair.

Slave Quarters near Harrisonville, Baltimore County, Md. Maryland Historical Society.

African Americans played a major role in the life of colonial towns that were growing in importance by the middle of the eighteenth century. Annapolis, which replaced St. Mary's City as the colonial capital in 1694, had a population of 1,000 by the middle of the eighteenth century. The colony's elite visited there during sessions of the General Assembly, and the capital became the cultural center of Maryland. African Americans in Annapolis worked not only as house servants but also in various businesses and shops, in skilled crafts, and in services such as those needed to operate hotels and restaurants. In 1752, Baltimore had only two hundred residents, but it was beginning to grow. Researchers have not yet identified Baltimore's earliest African Americans, but clearly they were among the early residents. Oxford and Chestertown, like Annapolis and Baltimore, were colonial ports. Many African Americans worked in the ports and on the ships that sailed Maryland's rivers and the Chesapeake Bay.

In summary, as the eighteenth century passed its midpoint, nearly one-third of the colony's people were of African descent. They lived in all parts of Maryland, in the countryside as well as in towns. The colony's elite relied on African American workers to provide the wealth that also made them powerful. Although the majority lived in southern Maryland, where tobacco plantations formed the basis of the economy, and on the Eastern Shore, with its more diverse agriculture, blacks lived in central Maryland and on the western Maryland frontier as well. Diversification of skills meant employment in an ever-growing variety of occupations. Extended family networks played a major role in their lives. About 4 percent of the total African American population were free. With increasing numbers of both slaves and free men and women born in North America, most were native speakers of English. African Americans were among the oldest families in the colony.

The Revolutionary Period

From the 1770s to the end of the century, some major changes took place in African American history in Maryland and throughout North America. The Revolution and its aftermath, religious opposition to slavery, and changes in the economy all had an extensive impact. Many people of African descent seized the opportunity provided by the American Revolution to protest slavery and to determine their own fate. By 1800, African Americans in Maryland were moving in new directions that would continue during the nineteenth century.

As the American revolutionaries were talking about liberty and human rights, the discrepancy between that ethic and the institution of chattel slavery was not lost on African Americans. In several colonies, slaves petitioned legislatures for their freedom, which they asserted was a natural right of all human beings. At the outset of the conflict, most white Americans were thinking about liberty as freedom from political and economic control by England. They simply accepted black slavery as part of the way of life. Only a few groups, such as the religious Society of Friends—often called Quakers—viewed slavery as contrary to the law of God. War and other forms of social upheaval generally afford the opportunity for change, and many African Americans stood up at this time and struck out to better their own lives. The result was some freedom, although not equality, for many former slaves.

Even before independence was declared in July 1776, it was clear that African Americans were important in the growing conflict between the "patriot" leaders of the independence movement and the British. African Americans formed an important part of the total colonial population not only because of their numbers but also because of their economic role in American society. Without black labor the planters in the southern colonies, who were among the leaders of the Revolution, could not survive economically. The British seriously considered slaves and poor white farmers, who were also victimized by the wealthy plantation owners, as potential allies. In 1775 the British governor of Virginia, John Murray, Lord Dunmore, offered to free any slaves and indentured servants who would leave their patriot masters and join the British. Dunmore's goal was twofold: to fill his ranks and to deprive the planters of their labor force. Some slaves took this opportunity to fight for their freedom. As the word spread, men from southern Maryland escaped to join men from Virginia. During the course of the war, many African Americans moved behind British lines in the hope of obtaining freedom. Many who fought for or supported the British were freed. The British provided transportation out of the United States to places such as Nova Scotia, now a Canadian province, the Bahamas, or Trinidad in the British West Indies.

Dunmore's action led the American revolutionary government, the Continental Congress, to reverse its early prohibition against African American enlistment in the regular army. New England militias enlisted African American soldiers first. Several southern states never consented to arm their slaves or free African Americans whom they feared would rebel against slavery. Maryland, a border state, had African Americans in its fighting force, although regular army enlistments were not allowed until 1780, when white enlistments declined. African American soldiers served in non-segregated units as they had earlier in colonial militias. Most are not identified by race in the official army records, making it impossible to know exactly how many blacks did fight during the War for Independence, but clearly they numbered in the thousands. One such African American was a soldier named Thomas Carney, who probably came from Queen Anne's County.[9]

In Maryland, the first African American fighters served on ships. Black pilots sailed on the Chesapeake Bay and on Maryland's rivers. These sailors, who had worked on the water before the outbreak of the war, contributed their expertise and skills to the military effort. Black sailors also served on large warships. There is a 1777 record of two African Americans who sailed on Maryland's first warship, the *Defense*. The names recorded are "Negro Tom," a slave, and "Black Yankee."[10] Numerous African Americans used Maryland's waterways as an escape route. Wartime confusion and the presence of black pilots aided these escapes.

Most African Americans who participated in the war effort assisted the patriots. Even non-combatants, women and children as well as men, helped build local defenses when they were needed. At the rapidly expanding port of Baltimore, African Americans helped build new ships and took an active part in supplying materials for the American army and navy. Baltimore was one of the chief centers for military supplies and the port grew rapidly during this time. Many African American workers contributed to that significant growth.

When the various colonies declared independence from England, one of their first jobs was to set up a government. Each new state wrote a constitution. A number of these state constitutions reflected the recognition that the ideals of liberty contradicted the practices of the system of slavery. Northern states provided for a gradual end to slavery within their borders. Although Maryland shared a long border with Pennsylvania, where slavery was abolished, slavery continued to be lawful in Maryland until the Civil War. In fact, slaves were not the only unequal people in Maryland or the colonies in general. In Maryland during the years before the Revolution slaves, women, Native Americans, Catholics, and Jews could not vote or hold public office. Only free men who possessed sizable wealth could exercise full privileges of citizenship. Married women were not permitted to own property. Native

Americans who had survived exposure to the new diseases that came from across the Atlantic had been chased out of Maryland as white settlers took over their land. Many colonists hoped that independence would also bring greater equality among people, at least to the extent of improving their own group's status.

Generally the new state constitutions set up governments that were more representative than the colonial governments had been, but none of them granted political equality in the sense that we understand it today. Maryland's 1776 constitution did not outlaw slavery, but it did allow some blacks to exercise the franchise. The Maryland constitution of 1776 gave the vote to all Christian males, twenty-one or older, who owned a specified amount of property. No Jews could vote. No women could vote. A few black men who met the property requirement could and did vote. At least one African American ran for public office. In 1792, Tom Brown, a veteran who had fought for Maryland during the Revolution, announced his candidacy for one of Baltimore's two seats in the state House of Delegates. He declared in an advertisement in the September 24 *Baltimore Daily Advertiser* that "justice and equality will excite you to choose one Man of Colour to represent so many hundreds of poor Blacks as inhabit this town, as well as several thousands in different parts of the state."[11] He did not win, but after the first decade of the nineteenth century, no African Americans in Maryland could run for public office or vote until sixty years later.

Following the Revolution, many Marylanders protested that slavery was a moral wrong and should be abolished. In a notable article published on May 15, 1783, in the *Maryland Gazette*, a writer who called himself "Vox Africanorum" (the voice of Africans) asked how Americans who had just fought for freedom could tolerate "fellow creatures groaning under the chains of slavery." He wrote that everyone desired freedom, that freedom was everyone's natural right, and that greed was responsible for the perpetuation of American slavery. He concluded with a plea, "Ye fathers of your country; friends of liberty and of mankind, behold our chains! . . . To you we look for justice—deny it not—it is our right."[12]

Some white Marylanders agreed with Vox Africanorum. Opposition to slavery grew as did the number of manumissions. Quakers and Methodists prohibited slave-owning by their membership. Their religions taught that all people were equal in God's eyes. Most Quakers did free their slaves. Many Methodists did too, although the Methodist Church gradually backed away from its strictest prohibitions against slave ownership. These manumissions, following shortly after the manumissions for service in the war and escapes during the war, resulted in the growth of a sizable free black community in Maryland, especially in central Maryland and on the Eastern Shore.

Early Abolitionism in Maryland

Abolitionism in Maryland followed a slightly different course than it did elsewhere in the nation. Abolitionist activity surged during the post-Revolutionary years of the late 1700s and early 1800s. It continued in Maryland through the 1820s, when abolitionist sentiment in the southern states had all but disappeared. After that time, anti-abolitionist forces predominated in Maryland. Blacks had to escape out of the state to become active leaders in the movement. Most white abolitionists turned to alternative activities. Free blacks consistently sought an end to slavery and equal rights for all. Ministers often served as the voice of the community. It was a difficult juggling act to speak out for freedom and yet stay out of trouble at the same time.

Quakers and other reformers in 1789 founded the Maryland Society for Promoting the Abolition of Slavery and the Relief of Poor Negroes and Others Unlawfully Held in Bondage. This organization and others continued to fight to end slavery and to protect the rights of free blacks. The nation's first exclusively antislavery newspaper, *The Genius of Universal Emancipation,* was published by Benjamin Lundy in Baltimore in the 1820s. William Lloyd Garrison came to Baltimore as Lundy's co-editor. On the streets of Baltimore the New Englander Garrison encountered slavery and the slave trade firsthand, and it was here that he developed his firm belief that no compromise was possible, that all slaves had to be freed immediately and have full rights of citizenship. Lundy was beaten on the street and his attacker freed by a judge who said his antislavery articles had provoked a justified attack. Some white Methodists were imprisoned for advocating abolition, and General Assembly bills to end slavery always fell in defeat. Bills to prevent the forcible break-up of slave families also failed.[13]

The 1831 Nat Turner rebellion in neighboring Virginia brought an end to the abolitionist movement in Maryland. Slaveholders feared a similar rebellion in their state and considered slavery an effective means of racial control. African Americans were carefully monitored and could not speak out publicly in favor of abolition or lead protest actions for fear of losing their lives. The few local white abolitionists who remained active frequently were forced from their jobs and sometimes physically attacked. Abolitionism was not a major force in Maryland politics after 1831. African Americans did, however, continue to protest in every way possible the unequal conditions in which they had to live. African Americans and some whites alike participated in the escape network called the Underground Railroad. Maryland played an especially important role in the operation of the Underground Railroad. Black pilots and sailors on the Chesapeake Bay often carried escaping slaves to the northern end of the bay, just a short distance from Pennsylvania. Harriet Tubman became well known for leading groups up the Eastern Shore through Delaware and on to Pennsylvania. Escaping slaves could find sanctuary in churches and also in Baltimore's large African American community until it was safe to continue the journey north to freedom. Many stories of the

Underground Railroad and its Maryland connections are recounted by Benjamin Still in his memoirs, *The Underground Railroad.* African American Marylanders such as James W. C. Pennington, Frederick Douglass, Harriet Tubman, and Henry Highland Garnet fled this state and became leading spokespersons in the fight for abolition.

One alternative proposal that drew support from some free blacks, former abolitionists, and even slaveholders was the effort of the Maryland State Colonization Society to establish a colony in Africa for former slaves. In 1832 the Maryland organization split off from the American Colonization Society that had established chapters across Maryland in Anne Arundel, Prince George's, Montgomery, Frederick, Washington, Queen Anne's, Dorchester, and Talbot Counties as well as in Baltimore. Marylanders led the effort to establish a colony called "Maryland in Liberia" at Cape Palmas, roughly 250 miles down the coast from Monrovia, the capital of Liberia, named by American settlers in the 1820s. In November 1833 nineteen African Americans—women, men, and children—sailed from Baltimore for Cape Palmas. By the following year, the group had built twelve houses. By 1837, more than two hundred residents lived in the colony under Jamaica-born Governor John Brown Russworm. In 1847 some of the settlements of American-born immigrants (though not Cape Palmas) formed a republic that they named Liberia. Marylander Daniel Warner was Liberia's third president. African Methodist Episcopal minister Daniel Coker, also from Maryland, was a spiritual leader in Liberia and also in neighboring Sierra Leone.[14]

Most African Americans in Maryland and across the United States spurned the suggestion that they move to a place that they had never seen. One reason for this reticence is found in the wording of Maryland's charter of the colonization society, which provided for a board to supervise "the Removal of Coloured People."[15] The majority of Maryland's African Americans wanted freedom, equal rights, and a share of the prosperity in the land of their birth, in the country they had helped build from the very earliest days.

The Free African American Community

Despite the failure of statewide abolition, Maryland's free African American community increased significantly following the Revolution. In 1790, one in thirteen persons within the Maryland African American community was free. Refugees of African descent from St. Domingue (now Haiti) settled in Maryland in the early 1790s when they moved to the United States along with Haitian whites, who had fled the St. Domingue slave revolt. In 1810, one-third of all African Americans in Maryland, over 33,000 individuals, were free. By 1840, the state's free black population of 62,000 included two-fifths of all African Americans. In 1860, just before the outbreak of the Civil War, almost one-half of Maryland's black population of 171,000 were free. In that same year, 90 percent of all African Americans in Baltimore were free and Baltimore had the largest free black community in the nation.[16]

Maryland's free African American community differed from others in southern cities such as New Orleans or Charleston for several reasons. Many people became free when they ran away and simply blended into the existing population. Furthermore, in Maryland, most manumissions were based on religious beliefs or economic conditions. But in the South many people were manumitted because of kinship with whites. Maryland's free blacks were less likely to be racially mixed and also were less likely to have been given land or any other property. Thus Maryland's free African Americans generally were not as wealthy as were the most prosperous southern free African Americans. Additionally, the free and slave communities in Maryland were less separated than were those in southern states.[17]

$100 REWARD.

RANAWAY from the Subscriber, living in Prince George's County, Maryland, on Thursday, the 6th of October, Negro Man

LEWIS,

commonly called LEWIS BUTLER. Lewis is about six feet high, very dark mulatto, spare made, very long limbs, with very long feet and hands; clothing coarse Osnaburg shirt and trowsers, and other clothing not recollected. I will give Fifty Dollars if taken in the State or District of Columbia; if out of the State, the above reward, and reasonable charges, if brought home, or confined in any Jail so that I get him again.

THOMAS SNOWDEN, Jr.

October 19, 1825.

Advertisement, Reward for Runaway, Prince George's County, Md., October 19, 1825. Many slaves escaped successfully and blended into the free black population. Maryland Historical Society.

The free African American community retained its closeness to the slave community for many reasons. Free people often had slave relatives. In some cases, one spouse was free and the other a slave. In other cases, an adult who had received his or her freedom was the parent of children who were still slaves. Often, free African Americans worked long and hard to save the money needed to buy relatives so that they, too, might attain free status. Many free people of color stayed in the vicinity where they had lived as slaves, because their families were there. Others traveled to Baltimore where they could find a variety of jobs. Escaped slaves also made their way to the city because there they could disappear into the large free black population. Even in those days, cities offered a level of anonymity never possible in small towns or rural areas.

A number of people of African descent in Maryland were neither completely enslaved nor completely free. Some slaves were "hired out" by their masters. In those cases, the owner essentially rented the slave to someone else, and payment for the slave's work went to the owner. Before long, some slaves could hire themselves out. They had to pay the owner a certain sum of money each week. With the rest, they paid for their own lodging, food, and other expenses. They often could save money to purchase their own freedom. There were also "term slaves" who had a legally binding agreement that they would become free after a certain number of years. All these various conditions worked to undermine the system of slavery.

Free African Americans were working people. In the cities and towns, the majority of the men were laborers. Most women worked out of economic necessity and were housekeepers or laundresses. In rural parts of the state, many men, women, and children were agricultural workers. Some became skilled workers or craftspeople, and a few owned their own businesses. Many blacks worked in skilled crafts such as blacksmithing, bricklaying, and carpentry. Others became barbers, butchers, cooks, sawyers, seamstresses, and shoemakers. Some men worked in Maryland's shipyards, often as caulkers. Others worked on the water harvesting oysters or as part of crews on ships sailing the Chesapeake Bay. Others worked as stevedores, loading and unloading ships. Some carters and draymen owned their own cart and horse or mule and made their living carrying goods from one place to another. African Americans dominated the catering business in many Maryland towns.

In the towns, especially Baltimore and Annapolis, a small number of African Americans owned successful businesses, while others, including ministers and teachers, were in the professions. In Annapolis, William Bishop II operated a successful carting business and worked on the construction of the Naval Academy. Bishop invested his profits in real estate. By 1860, he was the wealthiest African American in the city and the twelfth wealthiest man in the entire population of Annapolis.[18] In Pocomoke on the Eastern Shore, Captain Robert Henry was a successful shipowner and trader.[19] In Baltimore, a free African American artist named Joshua Johnson painted portraits of some of the city's leading citizens. Today his portraits are on display at museums in different parts of the nation. During the antebellum period Lewis Wells practiced medicine in Baltimore. Maryland's wealthiest African American resident in 1850 was Thomas Green, a Barbadian immigrant, who owned a barber shop in Baltimore on Light Street. Green invested his profits in real estate and, at his death in 1858, had a total worth of $17,000. His wealth was great enough that he took his family for extended vacations in the fashionable town of Saratoga Springs, New York. By 1860, 348 free African Americans in the city of Baltimore had accumulated $449,138 in property. Seventy women were among these property owners.[20]

As the number of free African Americans increased, limitations on their freedom grew more severe. They could go to court, but they could not testify against whites. As immigrants from Europe began to arrive in large numbers during the 1840s, they saw free blacks and also slaves as competitors for jobs. There was violence against black workers. Free blacks were required to have special licenses to operate certain businesses. As the newcomers gained political power, economic restrictions against blacks increased. Some jobs were reserved for whites only. Laws guaranteeing the right of assembly did not apply to African Americans in most parts of the state where they often could not hold meetings without whites being present. At one point, Maryland passed a law requiring any African American gaining freedom to move out of the state. This law was not widely enforced.[21]

Free African Americans proved that the basic premise of the defenders of slavery was wrong. They proved that African Americans could live independently. Furthermore, the number of escapes proved that they wanted to live independently. Slave owners who supported the Maryland State Colonization Society were correct in their perception that the free African American community posed a threat to the institution of slavery. Free African American men and women purchased their relatives and made them free. They taught slaves to read and helped them escape. Free African Americans throughout the state established churches, schools, and other important community institutions. Most importantly, these men and women stood as proof that freedom was possible.

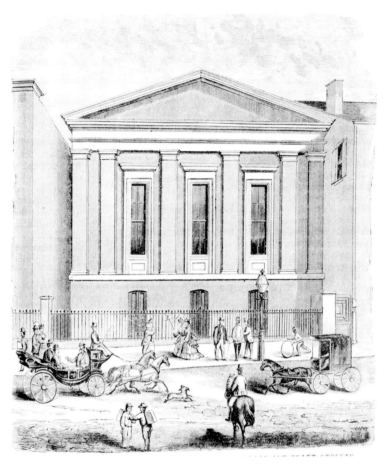

Engraving, "Sharp Street M.E. Church (Colored) Between Lombard and Pratt Streets." From George W. Howard, The Monumental City: Its Past History and Present Resources, *1873.*

The Nation's Largest Free African American Community

Baltimore's large antebellum African American community can list many accomplishments to its credit. With the largest free African American community in the nation, including both slave and free states, Baltimoreans were in a position to build institutions that would serve as examples and also set the stage for the future. Free blacks built churches, schools, and fraternal and self-help organizations that in some cases served the entire African American community. Local leaders rose to national prominence. This community and its leadership laid the groundwork for continued development in the period following the Civil War.

Churches were of vital importance in the African American community in Baltimore and throughout the state and country. Religion held a position of major significance in people's lives. Early slaves sometimes attended their masters' churches while maintaining beliefs and practices they had brought with them from Africa. Over the years, some became true converts to Christianity. This trend accelerated during the Great Awakening of the middle 1700s when new evangelical denominations emphasized the spiritual and emotional rather than the intellectual and liturgical elements of religion. Throughout the colonies, Methodists and Baptists appealed directly to slaves and free blacks. They encouraged people of African descent to join them. They preached that all people were equal in the eyes of God and that all might enjoy salvation.

In Maryland during the 1760s, a preacher known as "Black Harry" Hosier traveled with other early Methodist leaders. By 1765, Methodists had built at least two churches in Baltimore, on Lovely Lane and Strawberry Alley. For a while both had integrated congregations. Methodist leaders preached against slavery and at a conference in Baltimore in 1780 required that all in official church positions free their slaves. Methodist ministers would perform marriages not only for free blacks but also for slaves, at a time when slave marriages were not legal in Maryland. Roman Catholic priests also performed slave marriages.[22]

As the years passed, Methodism became less egalitarian. Although the church passed a resolution at a meeting in Baltimore in 1784 that all Methodists should free their slaves, some slave owners refused. Some people put pressure on Methodists to stop treating African Americans as equals. Soon, black worshipers were forced to sit in the back rows of church pews or in the balcony. They had to wait to take communion until after all the whites had finished. Church classes were segregated by both race and sex. In Baltimore, African American Jacob Fortie began holding prayer meetings in his home. These meetings eventually led to the building of the Sharp Street Methodist Church. This still was not a satisfactory situation for everyone because Sharp Street was subject to the overall leadership of the white-controlled Methodist church. Consequently some of the leaders from Sharp Street left that church and founded the African Methodist Bethel Society. Daniel Coker was a leader in the movement for an independent black church. In 1816, he took part in the conference in Philadelphia that established the African Methodist Episcopal Church. Bethel A.M.E. Church in Baltimore was the first black independent church in any of the states where slavery was legal.[23]

Baltimore African Americans worshipped in churches of other denominations as well. In 1824, William Levington, the third black man in the United States to be ordained an Episcopal priest, founded St. James Episcopal Church. At St. James, both free and slave male members could vote for church officers.[24] Congregations of black Baptists, Presbyterians, Roman Catholics and others also worshipped in Baltimore before the outbreak of the Civil War. All these churches were important to the community in many ways. In the churches, African Americans were the leaders. African Americans kept the financial records, decided on expenditures, wrote the sermons, planned the lessons and activities, and directed all the operations of the church. Some churches maintained libraries. Many organized mutual aid and burial societies. Churches provided a place for people to meet. In Baltimore and Annapolis, churches and several other groups, such as Masonic organizations, were exempt from the Maryland law that required a white person to be present at all meetings of African Americans.

Providing a school was one of the most important functions that many churches assumed. Before the city opened public schools for white students—which happened on a very small scale in 1829—black churches, and also white churches, operated day schools and Sabbath schools to teach the rudiments of reading and writing, sometimes math, and other subjects. African Americans saw that education was a way out of bondage and poverty, and many working adults as well as children sacrificed their precious free time to study. The African Academy that opened at the Sharp Street Methodist Church in 1802 led the way in making education available to African Americans, to free people and slaves, children and adults. When Daniel Coker began teaching at the African Academy in 1809 he attracted large numbers of students. By the time he left, over 150 pupils were coming to study there, some from as far away as Washington, D.C. Coker taught not only reading, writing, and math but also classical literature and history. He also taught racial pride and openly advocated emancipation. When Coker departed in 1820, many students studied with William Watkins, who became known for his excellent, effective, and difficult classes. Another Baltimore teacher, William Lively, operated the Union Seminary in Fells Point where he taught French and Latin in addition to the basic subjects. The Oblate Sisters of Providence, founded by nuns who had come from St. Domingue, opened a school for girls that was highly successful and drew young women from families across Maryland and from Washington, D.C. Baltimore's many black schools often suffered from lack of funds and other problems. Despite the hard battle they fought, their effectiveness can be gauged by the fact that the 1860 census listed as literate almost 55 percent of the city's free blacks over the age of twelve.[25]

Engraving, "Twenty-Eight Fugitives Escaping from the Eastern Shore of Maryland." The slaves were inspired and given directions by Harriet Tubman. Maryland Historical Society.

As the United States approached the Civil War, Baltimore's large black community and African Americans across Maryland were in a position to lead the fight for freedom and equality in the years that followed. Although most were not wealthy, many people, especially in Baltimore, were literate and had experience in community leadership. Some were prominent in business, religion, and education. None, even the most prosperous, had anywhere near equal rights. All hoped for a better life for themselves and for the entire black community.

The Civil War and Reconstruction

In Maryland, as in the rest of the United States, people went to war for many different reasons. For African Americans the clear goals were to end slavery and to realize the promise of full citizenship that black abolitionists and a few radical whites had urged for years. Across the North, some whites fought for that same goal. Others fought to bring the seceding states back into the Union, to prevent the break-up of the nation. Some were concerned primarily with economic issues. Across the South, some fought to preserve the plantation system of economics, including slavery, and to prevent northern domination of their economy. Many saw slavery as a system of racial control. Others in the South fought merely because the Yankees were there. For many people, both northerners and southerners, slavery was the one issue on which there could be no compromise. Either slavery would continue to be legal or slavery would be abolished. This was the moral issue that stirred passions. Without the dispute over slavery it is probable that compromise would have been possible and there would have been no war.

Maryland was in a unique position as the country approached war. Because of the state's geographic location between the North and South, many Marylanders wanted to avoid the fighting that almost surely would take place in the state. Others wanted to avoid a war between the states for business reasons. Men who did business with the South did not want that business cut off. Nor did men who had business with the North want to secede from the Union. Some slaveholders wanted to protect their property by helping the Confederacy. Others actually were Unionists. Many white Marylanders wanted peace above all else. That was not to be. As war broke out some Marylanders moved South to join the Confederate troops, but the majority chose the Union side. The presence of federal troops in the state reinforced that choice.

African American women and men chose freedom and took action in many different ways to reach that goal. Initially, both the United States Congress and the Maryland General Assembly refused to abolish slavery. Congress did end slavery in the District of Columbia during the spring of 1862. A steady stream of slaves left Maryland for Washington—sometimes hundreds a week. Many of those came from nearby Prince George's and Montgomery Counties. Congress also passed a law that forbade Union commanders from returning any fugitive slaves who came behind their lines.

Many slaves took advantage of the opportunity to gain freedom in this way. Early in the war, the Union army would not accept black soldiers. Especially in southern Maryland with its large black population, whites were reluctant to arm African Americans. However, when it was clear that Union victory was not going to happen in just a few months, Congress and Maryland rethought their positions and invited African Americans to serve, with the promise of freedom for themselves and their families at the war's end.[26]

Marylanders and black men from across the nation responded eagerly to the call. Around 200,000 African Americans fought with the Union army and navy. Six black regiments, with almost 9,000 men, fought from Maryland. Enlistments were rapid, despite the fact that black soldiers received unequal treatment. They received lower pay than white soldiers, had to serve in segregated units under white officers, and often were given inferior weapons. The Union navy accorded black sailors better treatment. They worked, lived, and ate in integrated units and were eligible to receive promotions. These Marylanders, with their knowledge of the local waters, proved valuable additions to the navy. By the war's end, over twenty African American soldiers and sailors had been awarded the Medal of Honor, the nation's highest military honor. Several recipients were from Maryland, including Sergeant Major Christian Fleetwood and Private William H. Barnes.[27]

African American civilians, both men and women, actively supported the fighting men and helped former slaves. Women, including Harriet Tubman, as well as men served as spies and communicated valuable information to the Union side. Women gave soldiers uniforms and medical care, and provided food and shelter for former slaves who had become refugees. They taught skills to assist people in finding jobs. Community leaders spoke out continuously, pressing the federal government to enlist black troops, abolish slavery, and grant the right to vote.[28]

President Abraham Lincoln's Emancipation Proclamation in 1863 ended slavery in all states in rebellion against the United States. Because Maryland had not seceded, the Emancipation Proclamation did not apply in Maryland. Maryland abolished slavery within its borders in a new constitution that went into effect in 1864. The Maryland document declared that "Hereafter, in this State, there shall be neither slavery nor involuntary servitude, except in punishment of crime whereof the party shall have been duly convicted, and all persons held to service or labor as slaves are hereby declared free."[29] The new constitution was approved by a majority of the state's voters and went into effect on November 1, 1864. At sunrise on that day, guns fired at Fort McHenry announced emancipation. African Americans throughout Maryland celebrated the freedom for which they had hoped, worked, and fought over the years.

Emancipation and the end of the war did not bring to fruition the hopes of Maryland's African Americans. Although slavery was illegal and former slaves were legally free, there were many disappointments. Few of the hopes for political equality, educational opportunity, economic improvement, and

"Baltimore's African Americans Celebrate the Fifteenth Amendment (1870) Establishing the Right of Suffrage." Maryland Historical Society.

societal change were realized. Although the 1864 constitution disenfranchised former Confederates by requiring an oath of past loyalty, Maryland legislators passed laws to restrict blacks' freedom and failed to pass laws that would promote improved living conditions. The end of the war brought a cessation of fighting but it did not end racist practices.

Some white Marylanders tried to keep slavery alive in devious ways. They forced former slaves to sign contracts to work for the rest of their lives. The courts sold some blacks convicted of petty crimes into service for terms ranging from six to eighteen months. Former masters forced children to become unpaid apprentices. African Americans were forbidden from testifying in court against whites so they generally had no recourse if they received wrongful treatment. African Americans' freedom to travel was limited as was the right to free assembly. Maryland approved another new constitution in 1867. This document restored the franchise to former Confederates, while continuing to refuse it to blacks. It was clear that change would not come through state legislation but rather from the efforts of the black community—with help from some white allies—and through the work of the federal government.

Some former slaves voluntarily remained in the rural areas where they had always lived. Others remained because they could see no other choice. Many people flocked to nearby cities, Baltimore and Washington, D.C., as well as smaller towns across the state. Poverty was a common problem, and jobs were not easy to find. Lack of education and lack of experience in urban ways made the search difficult for many former slaves, especially those from southern Maryland. Racial discrimination meant that blacks were often the last hired and first fired and generally received the lowest salaries. Poverty in the city and poverty in the country both caused misery. It was a major problem for many individuals and for the community as a whole.

Education had long been seen as a way out of poverty and repression. African Americans struggled to provide access to education. Maryland's first public schools, which began opening in the late 1820s and early 1830s, did not allow black students. The racial restriction had not changed at the time slavery ended. Churches carried the burden of education before the Civil War. During the war, a local organization with a typically long nineteenth-century name, the Baltimore Association for the Moral and Educational Improvement of Colored People, began to operate schools around the state. Privately funded, the association hired both black and white teachers, many of them women, who taught children and adults during the day and at night. Local African Americans and sympathetic whites raised the money for school buildings. In 1865, the association operated seven schools in Baltimore City and eighteen in Maryland's counties. Two years later, the organization maintained over one hundred schools on a budget of $76,000. The association founded a normal school to train black teachers; this eventually became Bowie State College. As the war ended, the federal Freedmen's Bureau began to operate schools in Maryland. The bureau also provided wood and other building materials to local groups to use in school construction. These efforts were not always welcomed by whites. Eleven schools for black children were destroyed by arson. The African American community persisted, despite the opposition. In 1867 Baltimore City, and subsequently the county governments, agreed to use school taxes paid by blacks to fund schools for black students. Shortly thereafter, money from general funds supplemented the small amount collected by the school taxes. Finally African American children could attend public schools in Maryland.[30]

Education continued to be a primary focus of the African American community. The first schools served only elementary-level students. Constant work finally resulted in the 1883 opening of the first high school in the state for black students. This became Frederick Douglass High School in Baltimore. In 1867, the Methodist Conferences of Baltimore, Washington, and Wilmington sponsored the Centenary Biblical Institute to train ministers. Soon it also trained teachers and then added a liberal arts program. Today that small college has become Morgan State University. Not until 1900 did the Baltimore Board of School Commissioners establish a normal school for African American teachers. This was later renamed in honor of Fannie Jackson Coppin, the first African American woman to earn a college degree, in 1926.[31] It is worth noting that a few African Americans in the 1880s attended the state's leading institutions of education, including the Johns Hopkins University and the University of Maryland, before the rigid segregation laws took effect. After that time, those schools remained segregated until change began gradually in the 1930s and 1940s.

The right to vote was another main focus of efforts during the years following the Civil War. African Americans in Maryland regained the franchise with the passage of the Reconstruction amendments to the Constitution of the United States. The Maryland General Assembly refused to pass legislation enfranchising black men (no women of any race voted until the passage of the Nineteenth Amendment in 1920) during the postwar years. It also refused to ratify the amendments to the U.S. Constitution that made African Americans full citizens of the United States and guaranteed the right to vote. Despite Maryland's reluctance, when the Fifteenth Amendment was passed and ratified by three-fourths of the states, it went into effect nationwide. All men in Maryland over the age of twenty-one, native-born or naturalized, had the right to vote. On April 8, 1870, Elijah Quigley of Towson became the first African American to vote in Maryland since 1810.

By fall 1870, over 35,000 African Americans had registered to vote. Most voted for the Republican Party. One of the major thrusts of African American leaders was to protect that right to vote through years of attempts to take it away. Marylanders succeeded in protecting their franchise when southern African Americans generally did not. The story is a fascinating case study in American politics. When state Democrats, hoping to dislodge the Republicans from office, tried three times to pass a literacy test requirement, the bill was defeated in a referendum. An interesting and unusual coalition that included black and white Republicans, reformers of both parties, and Democrats who were recent immigrants—or who depended on the immigrant vote—joined together to oppose the literacy test. The test was defeated, and African Americans continued to vote in Maryland during the years when most other states that had significant black populations had few, if any, black voters.[32]

Although African Americans in Maryland successfully defended their right to vote, they could not prevent the passage of a number of segregation laws around the turn of the century when states farther south were putting the same laws into practice. Many public institutions and places were segregated: schools, theaters, restaurants, hotels, and many stores, parks, and even cemeteries. Segregation, however, was not as uniform as it was in the South. Urban and western parts of Maryland were less segregated than southern Maryland and the Eastern Shore. A lawsuit by a visitor from New York desegregated the local Baltimore transit system, but trains statewide contin-

ued to run separate cars for African American and white passengers. Baltimore City housing segregation laws were challenged in court and were rejected because they limited an individual's right to dispose of his own property. But some neighborhoods had covenants that restricted buyers to whites
(or, in some cases, whites who were not Jews). Thus, by covenant or by
custom, many communities were closed to African Americans. Enoch Pratt,
on the other hand, when giving money for the public library in Baltimore,
specified that all people, regardless of their race or religion, who could read
and care for the books should have access to the facility. Many southern
regions denied black readers admission to public libraries.

During these difficult years, the African American community built im-
portant institutions. Baltimore, with its large population, continued to be a
focal point, as it had been during the antebellum period. In 1892, John
Murphy combined three small newspapers and began publishing the *Afro-
American*, which became one of the leading black newspapers in the country.
In 1894, three local African American physicians, William T. Carr, John Marcus
Cargill, and William H. Thompson, opened Provident Hospital. Although a
number of Baltimore hospitals did admit black patients to segregated wards,
at Provident African American physicians could treat their own patients in a
facility they owned and managed. Furthermore, African American nurses
were employed and later trained at Provident. During these same years, African American lawyers opened offices in Baltimore and entrepreneurs
founded and expanded a wide variety of businesses.[33]

Annapolis, although smaller, saw similar developments. William Butler, a
successful carpenter and landowner, was elected to the Board of Aldermen
in 1873, making him the first African American to hold public office in
Maryland. Dr. William Bishop, grandson of the man with the successful carting business, graduated from Howard University Medical School and returned home to practice medicine. He was one of the founders of the Annapolis Emergency Hospital and was also listed as a member of the hospital
staff. He assured that black patients would be admitted. Another Annapolitan,
Wiley Bates, a successful grocer and coal merchant, worked for many years
to improve education for African Americans in Anne Arundel County.[34] The
county's first high school for African American students was named for him.
On the Eastern Shore, in the town of St. Michael's in Talbot County, William
H. T. Coulbourne and Frederick S. Jewett opened a very successful seafood
company. They owned a fleet of work boats and built a cannery. For a time
during the 1920s the company of Coulbourne and Jewett was the largest
employer in Talbot County's history.[35] Despite massive legal discrimination,
some African Americans enjoyed great professional success. Schools, newspapers, medical facilities, law offices, businesses, and churches all expanded
employment opportunities for African American professionals while adding
jobs for working-class individuals as well. The educated men and women
who operated these institutions and businesses formed an elite leadership
that could and did fight on behalf of the entire community.

In summary, the decades following the Civil War saw the emergence in Maryland of a new generation of African American leaders who built on the foundations established by their antebellum predecessors. These men and women acquired good educations, built important institutions and businesses, and participated actively in state and national politics. They led the black community in a continuing struggle for economic development and full equality.

The Early Twentieth Century

As the twentieth century began, African Americans across the nation were suffering some tragic setbacks. Throughout the South, the last years of the nineteenth century and first years of the twentieth century were a time of disenfranchisement, segregation, and serious threats to physical safety in a society that had grown less concerned with racial justice. National political leaders were less interested in African Americans than they had been in the immediate aftermath of the Civil War. Republicans had turned their major focus to business and industrial expansion. This allowed southern Democrats to take back the political control they had lost when the Confederacy was defeated. These Democrats, seeking to ensure their continuation in power, disenfranchised most African Americans, who usually voted Republican, by instituting a system of poll taxes, literacy tests, and "grandfather" clauses to exempt those whites whose grandfathers had possessed the right to vote. When those devices failed, racists often turned to raw violence. As African Americans lost the vote in most states that had large African American populations, *i.e.* the former slave states, they also lost what national political influence they had during the decades after the war. Furthermore, in many communities, including places in Maryland, people were unable to protect themselves against viciousness, and organizations such as the Ku Klux Klan were free to inflict violence and terror. Lynch mobs often went unhampered by the local police and unprosecuted by the judiciary.

Maryland was one of the few states in which large numbers of African Americans continued to vote. The northern states had only small black populations. The states farther south had passed disenfranchisement measures. The cities of Baltimore and Annapolis, which had election districts with large black and/or Republican majorities, did continue to have African American representation in local government. So did Cambridge on the Eastern Shore. In Baltimore, six black Republicans sat on the city council between 1890 and 1931. Among these were Harry Cummings, Dr. John Marcus Cargill, Warner T. McGuinn, and William Fitzgerald.[36] In Annapolis, the African American community elected William Butler alderman in 1873 and successors William Butler, Jr., Wiley Bates, and Thomas Arrington Thompson.[37] A small number of all-black towns elected local officials such as Jeremiah Townshend Hawkins, who became mayor of North Brentwood in Prince George's County in 1914. The elected officials fought hard to protect the rights of their constituents and to gain public services for their districts. They did not always succeed, but their efforts certainly helped the general condition.

In addition to elected officials, other individuals and institutions fought hard for the black community. The Baltimore chapter of the National Association for the Advancement of Colored People was founded shortly after the formation of the national organization in 1909. Over the years, other branches opened in counties across the state. The Prince George's County chapter, for example, was begun in 1935 by Hester King, who served as its president for twenty-seven years. A Baltimore branch of the National Urban League was founded in 1924. The *Afro-American* newspaper, headquartered in Baltimore, provided a respected voice for community news and issues. The *Afro*'s owners and editors did not hesitate to speak out about injustice in its many forms. Organizations of clergy, lawyers, business people, teachers, and other professional groups also worked for full protection of the law, equal rights as citizens, and economic opportunity.

African American women's organizations took a leading role in pressing for reform. Maryland chapters of national organizations such as the National Association of Colored Women and the Alpha Kappa Alpha sorority joined local groups such as the Cooperative Women's Civic League in fighting on many fronts. Women such as Vivian Johnson Cook and Ida Cummings led these efforts. One major concern was the vote. In Maryland, neither black women nor white women could vote until the Nineteenth Amendment to the U.S. Constitution took effect in 1920. Black and white women worked separately and together on women's suffrage. African American women also worked hard for better health and sanitary conditions, for improved education, on children's issues, and against lynching. From the ranks of these African American women reformers came some of the first professionally trained social workers in Maryland, women such as Sarah Collins Fernandis and Anita Rose Williams.

Education was an urgent issue for the entire African American community. Politicians, ministers, staff writers from the *Afro,* and many others worked constantly to improve the education offered and the facilities available. They had to fight to get the state to open public schools for black children. Once there were public schools, they were segregated and unequal. The teachers were paid less than teachers in white schools. The buildings were older, often the old schoolhouses that remained when white students got new buildings. Books also tended to be secondhand, sent to black schools when white students got new ones. Still, teachers managed to provide an education and also were able to teach African American history and literature when this was not done in other schools. These teachers instilled pride in their students and stood as role models in the communities they served. For many years after Frederick Douglass High School opened in Baltimore City in 1882, it remained the only high school in the state for African American students. Most Baltimore African Americans who rose to prominence during the first half of the twentieth century attended Douglass. In the 1920s, one-third of all

Thurgood Marshall (left), working with Charles Houston, participated in his first high-profile case in 1935 when the NAACP represented Donald Murray (center). Murray won admission to the University of Maryland Law School in this landmark civil rights case. Library of Congress.

Douglass graduates went on to college or normal school. This was a very high percentage for any school at that time.[38] By 1921, across the state there were ten black high schools with about 300 students. As late as 1940, only 3.5 percent of all black children were able to complete high school.[39]

African Americans seeking a higher education also faced many challenges. Undergraduate degrees were available at several colleges. Morgan, Coppin, and Bowie served the community well. The University of Maryland, "white" state colleges, and the private colleges were closed to black students—for both undergraduate and graduate studies. Some students chose to go out of state, to places such as Howard University, Hampton Institute, Ashmun Institute (later Lincoln University), the University of Pennsylvania, and Columbia University. In 1935, Donald Murray, a young black man from Baltimore who had graduated from Amherst College in Massachusetts, applied to the University of Maryland Law School and was refused admission because of his race. The NAACP took the case to court and won. "Separate but equal" remained the law, but since there was no equal law school for black students in Maryland, the ruling came down that Murray would attend the University of Maryland. He graduated with an excellent record in 1938, the first black graduate in the twentieth century. The ruling was very limited and, until the 1950s, most African American graduate students still pursued their advanced education outside Maryland. Maryland's government took a number of steps to avoid integration in higher education. In 1935 the state purchased Princess

Anne Academy, which eventually became the University of Maryland on the Eastern Shore. In 1938, Bowie became a state teachers' college, and in 1939 the General Assembly voted to acquire Morgan College. The hope of many government officials was that if the state operated these facilities, they would not have to desegregate others. This strategy succeeded until the decade following the end of World War II.

In August 1914, World War I broke out in Europe. The United States joined the action in 1917 as an ally of Great Britain and France, who were fighting against Germany, the Austrian Empire, and the Ottoman Empire. The irony of the United States government's description of this as a "war to make the world safe for democracy" was not lost on African Americans, who had to fight to be able to fight. People in some parts of the nation were disinclined to arm black men. But pressure from black leaders and the needs of war did result in black participation. It took further efforts, on a national level, to get black combat units and officers' training units in the army. From Maryland, came 11,500 African American volunteers, 18.4 percent of the total.[40]

Eubie Blake (right) with Noble Sissle and Josephine Baker. Maryland Historical Society.

Some of the soldiers served in France where, for the first time in their lives, they saw a society without segregation. Many soldiers returned home unwilling to put up with the injustices of America's inequities.

The war had a profound impact not only on men and the few women in uniform but also on the civilian population. Large numbers of African Americans, and whites also, moved from rural areas into the cities to find well-paying jobs in war industries. Women as well as men provided welcome labor where minorities and all women had previously been excluded. Baltimore, Washington, D.C., and smaller Maryland cities were the destinations of people not only from rural Maryland but also from Virginia, North and South Carolina, and Georgia. Many of the migrants had little experience with urban life and came from states where education was even less available than it was in Maryland. Many were poor. Black families and individuals were forced by segregation to crowd into those urban neighborhoods where other blacks already lived. The overcrowding was extreme in many cases. Urban life often did not live up to its promise.

Little Willie's Cut Rate and Bar at the corner of Druid Hill Avenue and Whitelock Street is shown here in 1949. "Little Willie" Adams was an important businessman in the community. Henderson Collection, Maryland Historical Society.

The years immediately following the end of World War I were difficult across the nation. Veterans came home to look for jobs. Because war products were no longer needed, many of the war industries simply closed. Blacks and women lost their jobs first. Housing was scarce and most of the desirable neighborhoods had covenants that limited residence to whites only, in some cases to Christian whites, excluding Jews and many foreigners as well as African Americans. Some Americans reacted with bitterness to the lack of idealism in the peace agreement, which allowed France to punish Germany instead of "making the world safe for democracy." Many were angered and harmed by the lack of jobs and housing. Some looked for a scapegoat on whom to blame all the problems. Hate organizations increased all across the country. They targeted a wide range of people, with local victims depending, generally, on what groups were present in significant numbers or were active in the area. Some organizations threatened and organized violence.

The public's concern for physical safety was real. Throughout the 1920s the Ku Klux Klan burned crosses in Maryland and members marched with their faces hidden behind masks. In 1922 they marched in Baltimore and Frederick. In 1925 they marched in Baltimore and Hyattsville. The Klan of the 1920s was a quintessential hate group. Its leaders preached hatred not only of blacks but also of Catholics, Jews, immigrants, socialists and Communists, and they did their best to intimidate them all. African Americans were the primary victims of lynchings, which persisted in Maryland into the 1930s. Men were killed by lynch mobs in Salisbury in 1931 and in Princess Anne in 1933. These were signal events in the lives of many sensitive people. Not only were black men lynched, but the government authorities did not always try to protect them or to arrest the leaders of the lynch mobs. In 1933, when Governor Albert Ritchie sent 500 Maryland National Guard soldiers to arrest the mob leaders, local firemen turned the hoses on the soldiers.[41] All leaders of the African American community fought against this brutality and the system that allowed it to take place. Although Maryland did not suffer as much violence as some areas of the South, no amount was acceptable and black leaders, along with white allies, continued to fight against it until it became illegal. The NAACP and the *Afro* newspaper led the local protests against lynching and played an important role in the national campaign.

As the national economy improved and then boomed in the 1920s, there were more jobs, but African Americans continued to have a disproportionately high level of unemployment and employment in low-paying fields because of job discrimination. Despite the many problems, African Americans built a community culture of historic proportions. In Baltimore, African American professionals with some money lived in large, comfortable houses in the vicinity of Madison Avenue, McCulloch Street, and Druid Hill Avenue. Families where the adults had stable jobs also lived in that part of West Baltimore. The teenagers attended Douglass High School, which moved into a new building at the corner of Carey and Baker Streets in the mid-1920s.

Pennsylvania Avenue in Baltimore, a center of commercial and cultural life for decades, drew people from the city and surrounding counties. This photograph is from 1948. Henderson Collection, Maryland Historical Society.

Pennsylvania Avenue in West Baltimore became and for decades remained a cultural and economic center for African Americans from across the state. Blacks from counties near Washington, D.C. found the same sort of center there. From Anne Arundel and Baltimore Counties as well as the city and outlying areas, people streamed to Pennsylvania Avenue to shop and to go to the theaters and clubs. In the stores, African Americans could try on clothing, something most could not do elsewhere. The theaters featured the great entertainers including Pearl Bailey, Count Basie, Eubie Blake, Cab Calloway, Duke Ellington, Ella Fitzgerald, Ethel Waters, and Chick Webb. Tom Smith, a city Democratic leader, and Joe Gans, a champion boxer, opened hotels that catered to these entertainers as well as other African Americans who were traveling and who were not permitted to stay in most hotels. Beginning in the 1930s the Pennsylvania Avenue Merchants' Association sponsored an annual Easter Parade to which people came from near and far.

Baseball was a favorite pastime. Both the Negro Leagues and local semi-pro teams enjoyed a wide following. Teams such as the Cambridge Orioles, the Catonsville Social Giants, the Easton Blue Sox, and the team from the Lincoln Athletic Club in Ellicott City played before loyal fans. Negro League teams, the Black Sox and the Elite Giants, made their home in Baltimore in the 1920s, 1930s, and 1940s. They had great players. In 1922, playing with the Black Sox, Jud Wilson hit .467. Many famous men played for Baltimore over the years: Judy Johnson—born in Snow Hill on the Eastern Shore—also Roy Campanella, Junior Gilliam, Henry Kimbro, and Satchel Paige. Over the years, Baltimore's Negro League teams played exhibition games against white teams. Before racially mixed crowds, the black teams had 268 wins and 168 losses.[42]

The Baltimore Elite Giants shown in 1949, the year they won the National Negro League Championship. Included in this photo are top baseball players Joe Black (top row, left), Junior Gilliam (top row, second from right), Henry Kimbro (front row, fourth from left), and Leon Day (front row, far right). Babe Ruth Museum.

Most recreation was segregated. The public swimming pools that Baltimore City began to build were segregated. One pool for African Americans was built in Druid Hill Park. At this time Chesapeake Bay beaches were popular, and black Marylanders took day trips to Brown's Beach on steamers that traveled the Chesapeake Bay. Near the end of the nineteenth century, Frederick Douglass's sons, who were not permitted to enjoy the facilities at other resorts, bought land along the water's edge in Highland Beach in Anne Arundel County. This became a popular destination for middle-class and professional African Americans.

In this segregated society, people in the black community created and directed many of their own institutions. The largest organizations, although by no means the only ones, were in Baltimore. Gifted musicians Charles Harris and W. Llewellyn Wilson led Baltimore's City Colored Orchestra playing classical concerts. A. Jack Thomas organized the City Colored Band, whose members performed outdoor concerts during the summer. A YMCA on Druid Hill Avenue provided everything from a musical conservatory to day care. In 1935–36, black professionals organized the Monumental City Bar Association and the Monumental City Medical Association. Businessmen, teachers, insurance professionals, and others formed similar organizations. In the mid-1930s the city was home to more than 5,500 African American professional people, including the highest number of teachers in any United States urban school district. Throughout the state, churches large and small remained at the center of community life. Church suppers, church outings, church picnics, church meetings, and a host of other activities in addition to worship involved the majority of people.[43]

When the Great Depression hit Maryland in the 1930s, everyone was hurt. From coal miners in western Maryland to crab pickers on the Eastern Shore, many working people lost their jobs. Banks failed and took both

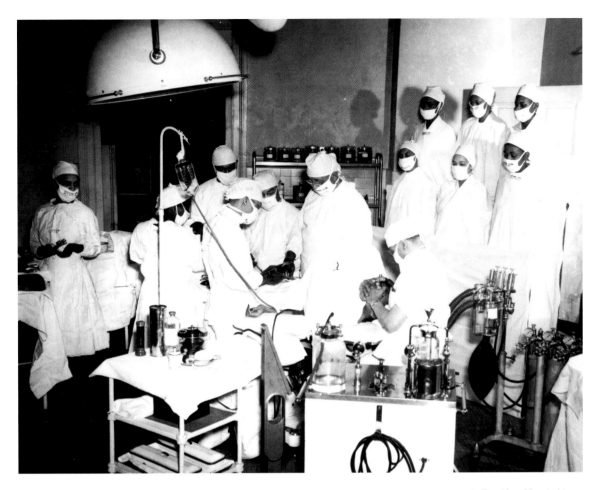

personal and business savings down with them. Some families lost their homes, and some people did not have enough to eat. Times were particularly tough for African Americans. Generally speaking, black workers and also all women were the first fired. These figures for Baltimore City are indicative of the problem. In 1933, 40 percent of the black population needed public support while only 13 percent of the white population needed that help.[44] In the town of Elkton, at one point during the Depression, two-thirds of all African Americans were without jobs.[45]

The dire economic situation sparked a number of responses from the black community. Leaders stood up to fight the discrimination that kept so many people poor. New organizations such as the Prince George's County chapter of the NAACP sprang into existence. Lillie Carroll Jackson, working with Carl Murphy, publisher of the *Afro*, rebuilt the Baltimore chapter of the NAACP, which then took a leading position in the fight for economic opportunity. An example of success was the agreement of the Baltimore City Police Department to hire African American officers, including Violet Hill Whyte. Whyte did the job of a social worker, helping the people in her community, as well as that of a law enforcement officer. It took a longer effort to convince the department to issue uniforms to black policemen and policewomen. Juanita Jackson, daughter of Lillie Carroll Jackson and a re-

At Provident Hospital in Baltimore, African American physicians and nurses treated patients from the community. This photo shows the operating room. Henderson Collection, Maryland Historical Society.

cent college graduate, founded the City Wide Young People's Forum, a group that met for intellectual, political, and social activities. Many young men and women who became Maryland's next generation of leaders worked together in the Young People's Forum. One joint activity of the Forum and the NAACP was a "Buy where you can work" campaign. Members carried picket signs along Pennsylvania Avenue where many of the non-black merchants were very happy to sell to black customers but would not hire black workers. A big victory came when the major food store, a part of the A&P chain, agreed to hire black cashiers to handle purchase transactions.[46] The NAACP, the *Afro*, and the black churches joined together to bring a lawsuit to equalize the salaries of black teachers with those of white teachers in the state. They won a court injunction, and equal pay for equal work became the law for teachers.[47]

A development of great political significance during the 1930s was the move of the majority of African American voters into the Democratic Party. The basis for this was economic. The New Deal of President Franklin Roosevelt not only offered aid to African Americans in need but also included black men and women in the government's various work programs. Agencies such as the Works Progress Administration taught both blacks and whites important job skills that helped unemployed individuals get work. The WPA and other agencies also hired crews to build public works projects that directly improved people's lives. For example, many rural areas got electricity for the first time. Some neighborhoods got sanitary sewers for the first time and people could abandon their outhouses for indoor bathrooms. Artists, writers, musicians, and historians got work through New Deal programs. A good number of talented African Americans were able to write, compose and perform music, paint or sculpt, and collect history during the 1930s. One project, particularly valuable to historians of the African American experience, was the collection of narratives from former slaves in which these men and women talked about their lives in slavery and in the years following the Civil War. If these stories had not been collected at this time, many of them would have disappeared as that generation of men and women died. Now they are available to all readers.

The Great Depression came to an abrupt end with the outbreak of World War II, which began in Europe in 1939. Even before American entry into this war following the bombing of Pearl Harbor in Hawaii in late 1941, American industries were supplying large amounts of war matériel to Great Britain and France. The war industries generated jobs, just as they had during World War I. The pattern repeated itself. Men and a number of women went off to war or to support the troops. People moved from farms and small towns to big cities to work in war industries. Soon there was full employment. African Americans and women were hired for jobs from which they had been excluded. The economy recovered quickly from the Depression.

The early World War II years saw some of the same problems that had risen early in World War I. African Americans had to protest in order to get

a fair share of the jobs. A. Philip Randolph threatened to lead a march on Washington if President Roosevelt would not issue an order requiring defense industries to use fair employment practices. Many Marylanders prepared to join this march. The order was issued and the factory jobs provided real opportunities for many people. One big contribution of African American civilians in Maryland was their work on the construction of the Liberty ships at Bethlehem Steel's Fairchild Shipyards. As was the case during World War I, black leaders had to fight the United States government for the right to serve under equal conditions in the armed forces, to have blacks trained as officers, and for black troops to be given combat assignments. The *Afro* was a major voice in this campaign. African American men and women from across the state joined in the war effort. Soldiers, sailors, nurses, and others served. Several Marylanders served with the prestigious Tuskegee Airmen, America's first black military fliers. During World War II, the African American goal was symbolized by a double "V"—victory over America's enemies abroad and victory over racism at home.

When World War II ended in 1945 the world was, in many ways, a different place. At the same time, in too many ways, life in America remained unchanged. As troops from the segregated armed forces returned home, the men and women going to southern states went home to legally segregated schools, segregated buses, segregated elevators, segregated hotels, restaurants, and theaters, and no right to vote. While legal segregation was not the law in the North, discrimination continued in housing, employment, and other important arenas of life. In Maryland segregation by law and by practice re-

Picketers protest the exclusion of African American patrons from Ford's Theater in Baltimore. Henderson Collection, Maryland Historical Society.

mained constant. Buses might not have been segregated, but schools and most public facilities still were. Maryland's servicemen who had fought against the racist Nazis returned home to the same separate and unequal world they had left. Furthermore poverty limited many lives to a struggle for survival. Poor housing, poor sanitation, poor jobs, and inferior educational facilities were the rule for many.

Something had changed though. African American leaders were determined to make the wartime ideals of liberty and equality apply to all Americans, and significant groups of whites joining African Americans were truly responsive to their demands. The acknowledgment of Hitler's racism forced many Americans of all backgrounds to see the discrepancy between America's stated democratic ideals and the real conditions of life in this country. For African Americans, the decades following World War II saw educational, economic, legal, and political advances of major proportions. By the end of the twentieth century much had changed, although many problems still remained.

As soldiers returned home from Europe and the Pacific in 1945, Maryland and the entire nation faced the same problems of unemployment and scarcity of housing that occurred after World War I. But this time, the federal government anticipated and tackled the problems. The 1944 G.I. Bill passed by Congress to help the returning veterans was extremely important. Under this legislation, the federal government paid for four years of education for everyone who had served in the military, black and white, female and male. Men and women who never had dreamed of the possibility went to college and some continued on in graduate programs. Others trained for skilled jobs such as auto mechanic, appliance repairman, or secretary. The G.I. Bill, a major piece of social legislation, took thousands upon thousands of people out of the work force while industry reconverted to peacetime production, which happened quickly. Furthermore, the government created jobs of all sorts as national financial resources supported programs to build new infrastructure, everything from roads to airports to housing. By 1947, the country enjoyed widespread prosperity.

While the nation as a whole began to enjoy better times, Civil Rights leaders fought with renewed determination to win the remaining half of the wartime "Double V"—victory over racism. The success of President Harry Truman's 1948 executive order integrating the armed forces showed what was possible with responsive and determined leadership. Maryland gained an effective and concerned executive when Theodore McKeldin became governor in 1951. In the year he took office, he established the Commission on Interracial Problems and Relations. African Americans and whites working with the commission established an effective channel of communication and helped realize the goals of Civil Rights activists. McKeldin appointed African Americans to most state boards and also appointed black magistrates to the courts. He ordered the state parks to be opened to all Maryland's people.

Much early post-war attention was focused on education. The national leaders of the NAACP made a decision to change its strategy and go after the "separate" aspect of "separate but equal," asserting that legally enforced segregation by its very existence would never be equal. Before any court decisions were handed down, several private colleges admitted black students. The Johns Hopkins University admitted Frederick I. Scott, Jr., in 1945 as an undergraduate. He graduated in the class of 1950.[48] St. John's College in Annapolis voluntarily admitted, in 1948, its first African American resident student, who graduated successfully four years later. In 1950 a lawsuit opened the University of Maryland School of Nursing to African Americans. The following year, the university's Graduate School admitted a black student without being forced by a lawsuit. In 1954, the prestigious Baltimore Polytechnic Institute accepted African American students a year before it was required to do so. During these same years, for the first time, a black officer was promoted to the rank of sergeant in the Baltimore Police Department, the first license was issued to an African American plumber, and African American doctors were allowed to see their patients in "majority" hospitals.[49]

The year 1954 was a turning point nationally and in Maryland. In May the United States Supreme Court handed down the *Brown v. Board of Education of Topeka* decision requiring that segregation by law end in all public schools across the country. Baltimore City and County and some other jurisdictions in the state hastened to comply. Other parts of the state, particularly several with large black populations, were considerably slower. The University of Maryland opened all its campuses to black students, admitting the

African Americans had to protest to gain access to public schools, to obtain equal pay for teachers, to gain access to equal facilities, and, in the end, to desegregate the schools. Henderson Collection, Maryland Historical Society.

first undergraduates to the College Park campus in September 1954. Maryland became the first state university below the Mason-Dixon Line to integrate its undergraduate student body, but black students were few in number and did not always feel welcome. The goal of equal educational opportunity was not fully realized. Generally, only a few students at all educational levels took part in the early integration and not all had pleasant experiences. This was only a beginning.

Another important new beginning occurred in 1954 when African Americans were elected to the Maryland General Assembly for the first time in the state's history. Harry Cole, running as a Republican, won election to the State Senate while Truly Hatchett and Emory Cole (no relation) went to the House of Delegates. All came from Baltimore's heavily Democratic and majority black Fourth Legislative District. In the following year, Walter Dixon was elected to the Baltimore City Council, the first black member since 1931. In 1958, Verda Welcome and Irma Dixon became the first black women in the General Assembly. From the 1950s on, black representation in state government grew and also came from increasingly wider cross sections of the state.[50] These representatives could speak for their constituents but, because of their small numbers, were able to influence legislation by their powers of persuasion but not by the number of their votes. This, again, was only a beginning.

The growth of the suburbs represented another important trend of the decade following the end of World War II. This was a movement in which most African Americans were not early participants. However, suburbanization had a major impact on everyone's lives. Roads were built leading out from Baltimore and Washington and from the state's smaller cities to areas that had recently been countryside. The Federal Highway Program helped pay for the new roads. Car manufacturers profited as people who could afford them purchased cars to reach these places that were not accessible by public transportation. Developers made fortunes building housing that was soon followed by shopping malls. Montgomery and Prince George's Counties grew rapidly, as did Baltimore and Anne Arundel Counties. Few of the new neighborhoods welcomed African Americans, even those who could afford to buy the houses. Many could not afford to buy homes, as most banks did not extend home loans to non-whites, even if those persons worked at regular jobs with good wages.

By 1954, after decades of migration from rural areas to the industrial cities, more than two-thirds of all African Americans in Maryland were living in urban areas. As white families moved away from the cities, a higher percentage of the remaining urban residents were African American. By 1958, 50 percent of students in Baltimore City schools were black. The racial "push" factor joined the "pull" factor of the spacious suburbs with modern houses in luring whites away from cities. A few black suburbs sprang up in the 1950s, such as Pleasant View with its ranch-style houses, north of Baltimore. But, generally, white middle-class families moved to the suburbs, leaving

African Americans and the poor behind. As businesses and jobs followed people to the suburbs, conditions in the inner cities deteriorated. Urban governments were left with serious problems and decreasing resources with which to handle them.

Meanwhile, the Civil Rights Movement continued. One major focus was on desegregating American life so that everyone, regardless of race or religion, could have equal access to all facilities. Montgomery County, which had a relatively small black population, opened all its restaurants in 1957. In 1960, shortly after the first lunch counter sit-ins in Greensboro, North Carolina, college students in Baltimore used the technique. Young men and women from Morgan State College, the Johns Hopkins University, and Goucher College sat in at the Northwood Shopping Center near the Morgan campus. Before that protest even the movie theater was not open to the students who lived across the street. Morgan students took the protest downtown as well, and many were arrested for their efforts. Other direct actions followed in Baltimore, College Park, Salisbury, and other locations. National leaders as well as students from a wide area took part in opening up the restaurants along Route 40, then the main driving route from Washington, D.C., to New York City. Dark-skinned diplomats traveling from Washington to the United Nations headquarters could not get a meal on the Maryland section of the highway. Even the State Department was pleased when this protest succeeded. In 1963, African American protestors were joined by white clergymen outside the Gwynn Oak Amusement Park in Baltimore County until it

The Afro-American *supported an annual Clean Block Campaign to foster neighborhood pride and preservation. Prizes were highly valued. Henderson Collection, Maryland Historical Society.*

was desegregated. For a long while, it seemed as if a separate protest would be necessary before each place and each facility opened up to everyone.[51]

In 1963, Gloria Richardson led a protest in Cambridge on the Eastern Shore. In this town with many old black families, including professionals, segregation was still the rule. Another big issue was the shortage of jobs. Economic inequalities affected life every day. When the action turned violent, some people were critical. More perceptive observers saw this as a beginning of a new wave of protest. That same year Civil Rights forces in Maryland won a major legislative victory. The state passed a Public Accommodation Law that opened restaurants, hotels, theaters, and other public facilities to all patrons. By 1965 a major effort was made to desegregate housing. Since much housing segregation was enforced by neighborhood covenants, by directed home sales, and by selective renting, more than a law was needed. Demonstrators picketed or sat-in at segregated apartment buildings. Housing testers got proof that a particular apartment owner's rental policy or realtor's sales policy was to exclude African Americans. Testers arrived in series of three pairs—white, black, and then white—to try to rent or buy the same apartment or home. If the place was available to both white couples but not to the African Americans who came in between, this fact was added to a body of evidence that would, with enough examples, prove illegal discrimination.

One community offered open facilities for everyone. Columbia, a planned community designed and built in Howard County by progressive developer James Rouse, deliberately encouraged people of all races and religions to come live there. From the beginning in 1963, all the suburban amenities were available to all residents. Here, blacks and whites had equal access to swimming pools, golf courses, well-equipped schools and, of course, new homes in nicely landscaped communities. Many African Americans moved to Columbia, often commuting to work in Baltimore and Washington.

The strong Civil Rights Movement won major victories on a national level. Marylander Clarence Mitchell, the head of the Washington office of the NAACP, played a leading role in this process. Congress passed and President Lyndon Johnson signed the Civil Rights Act of 1964 and the Voting Rights Act of 1965. Johnson undertook the War on Poverty with the worthy if exceedingly difficult goal of ending poverty throughout this wealthy nation. In the African American community, there was increasing awareness of the economic issues and disparities. The year 1965 also witnessed the growing conflict in Vietnam. The anti-war movement included many African Americans, among them Dr. Martin Luther King, who noted that there were high numbers of black soldiers in the infantry—units where they were most likely to be killed or wounded. In 1966 the Maryland State Advisory Commission to the United States Civil Rights Commission found "no meaningful desegregation" in schools in many of the state's counties, all in southern Maryland or on the Eastern Shore. Although no one could deny that a lot of things had changed, many people felt discouraged and angry that after all the

hard work of the past two decades so many problems and such enormous inequities remained. After Dr. King was assassinated in 1968, there were violent protests across the state and nation. The protesters made it clear that, although much had been accomplished, much still remained to be done. The law had desegregated many facilities for those people who could afford them, but poverty continued to plague the lives of many who could see no way out to a better life. Several decades of anti-poverty programs had not solved this problem by the end of the twentieth century.

While inner-city poverty continued, the African American middle class grew larger. The benefits of educational opportunities and the laws against job discrimination were being felt. Enjoying the fruits of their economic success, many middle-class people chose to move to the suburbs. During the last decades of the twentieth century, African Americans moved to Prince George's and Montgomery Counties next to Washington, D.C., and also to Baltimore County and Howard County. The movement away from the cities has continued as people move beyond these counties to places even farther out. Rebuilding in the urban centers has, however, attracted others back to the center cities, including many young professionals. As the twentieth century ended, there was no specific place in which blacks were expected to live. This diverse residential pattern had important political as well as social implications.

Beginning in the 1970s, African Americans made great gains in political

Thurgood Marshall, who became the first African American Supreme Court Justice, receives an NAACP award plaque from Carl Murphy. Henderson Collection, Maryland Historical Society.

power. More African American women and men were elected to government offices at all levels and, over the years, they acquired seniority. Also, increasingly, African Americans were elected to high offices, in both the legislative and the executive branches of national, state, and local government. Many African Americans were appointed and elected to judgeships during the 1970s and the decades that followed. All these officials have contributed to the course of the nation's and Maryland's history. Important to the African American community and important to all residents of Maryland, they have carried out their duties at many levels and in all regions of the state.

In 1970, Parren J. Mitchell was elected to the United States House of Representatives from the Seventh Congressional District. A graduate of Morgan State University with a master's degree from the University of Maryland, he was the first African American to represent Maryland in the U.S. Congress. Kweisi Mfume, also a Morgan graduate with a master's degree from the Johns Hopkins University, succeeded Mitchell in 1987. He served as chair of the Congressional Black Caucus from 1992 to 1994, and held his seat until 1996 when he resigned to become president and chief executive officer of the national office of the National Association for the Advancement of Colored People, now located in Baltimore. Elijah E. Cummings, a Howard University graduate with a law degree from the University of Maryland, then became the third African American to represent the Seventh District. While Mfume was in office, a second African American congressman was elected from Maryland, this time from the Fourth Congressional District in Prince George's and Montgomery Counties. Albert R. Wynn took his seat in Congress in 1994. Wynn is a graduate of the University of Pittsburgh with a law degree from the Georgetown University Law Center.

Increasing numbers of African American men and women represented their districts in the Maryland General Assembly. Here, as in the United States Congress, seniority led to positions of leadership. In the Maryland State Senate, Clarence W. Blount, a Democrat from the Forty-First District, became Majority Leader as well as chair of the Economic and Environmental Affairs Committee. In the House of Delegates, Howard "Pete" Rawlings became chair of the powerful Appropriations Committee and Hattie N. Harrison chair of the Rules Committee. By the turn of the century, not only Baltimore City and Prince George's County—with their large black populations—but many other counties as well sent state legislators to Annapolis in numbers large enough to have a major impact on legislation.

Several African Americans became chief executive officers in major local jurisdictions. Clarence "Du" Burns became Baltimore's first black mayor in 1986 when, as president of the City Council, he succeeded Mayor William Donald Schaefer when Schaefer was elected governor of Maryland. In 1987 Kurt L. Schmoke, a graduate of Yale University and Harvard Law School, won election as mayor of Baltimore and served three terms as the city's chief executive. Wayne Curry of Prince George's County, a graduate of the University of Maryland School of Law, became the first black chief executive of a Maryland county when he won election in 1994. Richard N. Dixon, a Morgan graduate whose home is in Carroll County, became Maryland's state treasurer in 1996. Also in 1996, Judge Robert M. Bell, a graduate of Morgan and of Harvard Law School, was appointed chief judge of the Maryland Court of Appeals by Governor Parris Glendening. He became one of very few African American chief judges in our nation. In 2002, Michael Steele became Maryland's first African American lieutenant governor.

In the last half of the twentieth century, a significant number of African Americans in Maryland rose to heights of achievement and success in a wide variety of professions. With success came substantial financial rewards for many. There are so many individuals in fields such as medicine, law, literature, art, education, business, sports, and entertainment that it is impossible to name them all in a brief survey. Their contributions have benefited all Maryland's people and are an important part of the state's recent history. The struggles of the Civil Rights leaders, the hard work of the women and men who provided them with a good education, the pioneering leadership of the men and women of earlier generations, and the abilities of these leaders themselves have all contributed to their success. They, in turn, are in positions to lead the African American community as well as the rest of Maryland in the twenty-first century.

References

[1] Robert J. Brugger, *Maryland: A Middle Temperament, 1634–1980* (Baltimore: Johns Hopkins University Press in association with the Maryland Historical Society, 1988), 43. See also Father Andrew White, *A Briefe Relation of the Voyage Unto Maryland,* Maryland State Archives 350th Anniversary Document Series (Annapolis: Maryland State Archives, 1990), for information on the trip and the various passengers. Little is known of the second African on board.

[2] Brugger, *A Middle Temperament,* 43; Ross M. Kimmel, "Free Blacks in Seventeenth-Century Maryland," *Maryland Historical Magazine,* 71 (1976): 21–22.

[3] Kimmel, "Free Blacks in Seventeenth-Century Maryland," 22–25.

[4] Silvio A. Bedini, *The Life of Benjamin Banneker: The First African-American Man of Science,* 2d ed., rev. and exp. (Baltimore: Maryland Historical Society, 1999), chapter 2 *passim.*

[5] Brugger, *A Middle Temperament,* 43–47; Jean B. Russo, "Maryland's Formative Years, 1634–1763," in Suzanne Chapelle et al., *Maryland: A History of Its People* (Baltimore: Johns Hopkins University Press, 1986), 24, 40–41.

[6] Alex Haley, *Roots: The Saga of an American Family* (New York: Doubleday Books, 1976), 724.

[7] Barbara Jeanne Fields, *Slavery and Freedom on the Middle Ground: Maryland During the Nineteenth Century* (New Haven: Yale University Press, 1985), 4–6.

[8] Brugger, *A Middle Temperament,* 62.

[9] Benjamin Quarles, *The Negro in the Making of America,* 2d rev. ed. (New York: Collier Books, 1987), 43–56; William L. Calderhead, "Thomas Carney: Unsung Soldier of the American Revolution," *Maryland Historical Magazine,* 84 (1989): 319–26.

[10] Gregory A. Stiverson, "The Revolutionary War Era, 1763–1789," in Chapelle et al., *Maryland,* 88.

[11] Christopher Phillips, *Freedom's Port: The African American Community of Baltimore, 1790–1860* (Urbana: University of Illinois Press, 1997), 83.

[12] Stiverson, "The Revolutionary War Era," 89.

[13] Brugger, *A Middle Temperament,* 167–69; John R. Wennersten, *Maryland's Eastern Shore: A Journey in Time and Place* (Centreville, Md.: Tidewater Publishers, 1992), 122.

[14] Brugger, *A Middle Temperament,* 212; Fields, *Slavery and Freedom on the Middle Ground,* 10.

[15] Brugger, *A Middle Temperament,* 212.

[16] Phillips, *Freedom's Port,* 15. For detailed statistics see also Fields, *passim.*

[17] Fields, *Slavery and Freedom on the Middle Ground,* 28–32.

[18] Bishop Family Papers, Maryland State Archives, Annapolis.

[19] Brugger, *A Middle Temperament,* 265.

[20] Phillips, *Freedom's Port,* 153.

[21] Fields, *Slavery and Freedom on the Middle Ground,* 35–37.

[22] Phillips, *Freedom's Port,* 119–23.

[23] Ibid., 125–29.

[24] Ibid., 140.

[25] Ibid., 163–67. See also Bettye Gardner, "Antebellum Black Education in Baltimore," *Maryland Historical Magazine,* 71 (1976): 360–66.

[26] Brugger, *A Middle Temperament,* 268–69, 299; Quarles, *The Negro in the Making of America,* 110–13.

[27] Jean H. Baker, "Maryland in Peace and War," in Chapelle et al., *Maryland,* 168–69; Brugger, *A Middle Temperament,* 301–4;

Quarles, *The Negro in the Making of America,* 118–21; Charles H. Wesley et al., *International Library of Afro-American Life and History: Afro-Americans in the Civil War* (Cornwells Heights, Pa.: Publishers Agency, 1978), 240. See also John W. Blassingame, "The Recruitment of Negro Troops in Maryland," *Maryland Historical Magazine,* 58 (1963): 20–29.

[28] Quarles, *The Negro in the Making of America,* 121–22.

[29] Quoted in Baker, "Maryland in Peace and War," 169.

[30] Brugger, *A Middle Temperament,* 308–9, 418; Suzanne Ellery Chapelle, *Baltimore: An Illustrated History* (Sun Valley, Cal.: American Historical Press, 2000), 140. See also Martha S. Putney, "The Baltimore Normal School for the Education of Colored Teachers: Its Founders and Its Founding," *Maryland Historical Magazine,* 72 (1977): 238–52, and Bettye C. Thomas, "Public Education and Black Protest in Baltimore, 1865–1900," *Maryland Historical Magazine,* 71, (1976): 381–91.

[31] Chapelle, *Baltimore,* 140–41.

[32] Margaret Law Callcott, *The Negro in Maryland Politics, 1870–1912* (Baltimore: Johns Hopkins University Press, 1969), *passim.*

[33] Chapelle, *Baltimore,* 166–67.

[34] Jean B. Russo, Historic Annapolis Foundation. Unpublished manuscript.

[35] Lamont W. Harvey, "Black Oystermen of the Bay Country," *The Weather Gauge,* 30 (Spring 1994): 4–13.

[36] Suzanne E. Greene, "Black Republicans on the Baltimore City Council, 1890–1931," *Maryland Historical Magazine,* 74 (1979): 203–22.

[37] Jean B. Russo, Historic Annapolis Foundation. Unpublished manuscript.

[38] Chapelle, *Baltimore,* 194.

[39] Constance B. Schulz, "Prosperity, Depression, and War, 1917–1945," in Chapelle et al., *Maryland,* 246.

[40] Ibid., 219.

[41] Brugger, *A Middle Temperament,* 476–77, 508.

[42] Jim Bready, *Baseball in Baltimore: The First 100 Years* (Baltimore: Johns Hopkins University Press, 1998), 159–83; Brugger, *A Middle Temperament,* 465.

[43] Brugger, *A Middle Temperament,* 520.

[44] Ibid., 520.

[45] Schulz, "Prosperity, Depression, and War," 234–36.

[46] Chapelle, *Baltimore,* 200–201.

[47] Schulz, "Prosperity, Depression, and War," 246.

[48] *Hullabaloo* (Baltimore: Johns Hopkins University, 1950). This yearbook has photographs of graduates as well as accounts of extracurricular activities.

[49] Brugger, *A Middle Temperament,* 568–73; Dean R. Esslinger, "Maryland Since World War II, 1945 to the Present" in Chapelle et al., *Maryland,* 287–88.

[50] Chapelle, *Baltimore,* 208.

[51] Brugger, *A Middle Temperament,* 599–610; Esslinger, "Maryland Since World War II," 289.

A Portrait Gallery

George "Father Divine" Baker

Religious Leader

1879–1965

George Baker was the most flamboyant and successful of the independent African American religious leaders flourishing in Harlem, New York, during the 1930s. Born in May 1879 in Rockville, Maryland, the eldest child of Nancy Smith Baker and George Baker, he was educated in the segregated school system of Montgomery County. As a young man he moved to Baltimore to develop his religious talents. He soon became well known as a preacher and faith healer but did not affiliate with any of the established African American churches in Baltimore. Instead, he was influenced by the views of Charles Fillmore's United School of Christianity and other "New Thought" religious groups. Within a few years, Baker became one of the most influential and enduring independent storefront preachers in Baltimore's African American community. He developed a close relationship with other Baltimore independent religious leaders, including Harriet Anna Snowden, Samuel Morris—who had declared himself to be "The Father Eternal"—and John A. Hickerson, who proclaimed himself the "Reverend Bishop Saint John the Vine." Together the leaders established a faithful following. However, in 1912, serious disagreements arose and they separated. Baker immediately launched his own independent movement.

Baker left Baltimore to preach in the South. He often spoke in tongues, and urged his audiences to sing, dance, and conduct Holy Communion banquets. He developed the "International Modest Code," which required "no smoking, no drinking, no obscenity, no vulgarity, no profanity, no undue mixing of the sexes, no receiving of gifts, presents, tips or bribes." Many African American clergy disliked him. He was thrown out of Christian churches for declaring that he was God and arrested in Savannah and Valdosta, Georgia, for his activities.

In 1930, Baker formally changed his name to "Major Jealous Father Divine." He gained influence, and in the 1930s New York City politicians courted his endorsement for their election campaigns. In the early 1940s he garnered 250,000 signatures on one anti-lynching bill. He also had a smaller but equally active following of white converts. Baker moved his headquarters to New York, first to Brooklyn, then to Harlem, and later to Long Island. But the Peace Mission was plagued by controversy. Followers would frequently be arrested for disorderly conduct at services, and the movement was accused of improper business deals and occasional sex scandals. In addition, the group was frequently under the scrutiny of mainstream churches, police, and government officials, as well as being the subject of several high-profile court cases. Adding to the controversy was the sudden death, in 1931, of a New York judge who had sentenced Divine and eighty followers to prison for disorderly conduct. The case added to Baker's notoriety. The Peace Mission was supported by member donations and by the establishment of various businesses and the weekly newspaper, *The New Day*. Baker lived lavishly, purchasing mansions beyond the reach of most Americans.

Baker's "New Thought" teachings promoted self-help, the promise of affluence for members, freedom from illness, and racial integration. His Pentecostal-like movement appealed to thousands of churchgoers, from the poor and the hungry to the wealthy. At its height, the Peace Mission Movement stretched from New York City to Los Angeles, with a membership—according to some estimates—of 60,000 followers.

Baker married twice. His first wife became known as "Mother Divine." After her death, in 1946, Baker married Ednah Rose Ritching, a white Canadian follower known as "Sweet Angel." "Father Divine" died September 10, 1965, of arteriosclerosis and diabetes.

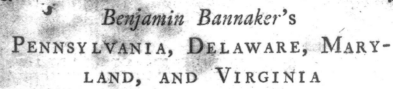

Benjamin Bannaker's
PENNSYLVANIA, DELAWARE, MARY-
LAND, AND VIRGINIA
ALMANAC,
FOR THE
YEAR of our LORD 1795;
Being the Third after Leap-Year.

○○○○ ○○○○ ○○○○ ○○○○ ○○○○ ○○○○ ○○○○ ○○○○ * ○○○○ ○○○○ ○○○○ ○○○○ ○○○○ ○○○○ ○○○○ ○○○○

BANNAKER.

○○○○ ○○○○ ○○○○ ○○○○ ○○○○ ○○○○ * ○○○○ ○○○○ ○○○○ ○○○○ ○○○○ ○○○○ ○○○○ ○○○○ ○○○○ ○○○○

—PRINTED FOR—
And Sold by JOHN FISHER, *Stationer.*
BALTIMORE.

Benjamin Banneker

Surveyor and Man of Science

1731–1806

Benjamin Banneker gained wide renown as a man of science, a naturalist, an able mathematician, and a creator of almanacs. Opponents of slavery publicized his abilities as evidence of the intellectual achievements possible for African Americans at a time when defenders of slavery claimed that blacks were mentally inferior to whites.

Benjamin Banneker was born on November 9, 1731, in western Baltimore County, near the present town of Oella. His father, Robert, born in Guinea, West Africa, had been captured, sold into slavery, and later freed because of his rebelliousness and his dignity. Benjamin's mother, Mary, was born in Baltimore County, the daughter of Molly Welsh, an English farm worker who had come to America as an indentured servant after her employer accused her of stealing milk, a crime for which she could have been put to death. She served out the term of her indenture, rented land, and began a farm that she eventually purchased. She bought two slaves to help her, soon freed both men and, despite laws discouraging the mixing of the races, married one of them, Bannaka, who had been born in Senegal. Mary and Robert initially lived at the farm, where Benjamin and his three sisters were born. Grandmother Molly provided the children's early education. In 1737, Robert bought one hundred acres of land and listed his son as co-owner. Young Benjamin briefly attended an integrated one-room Quaker school and helped with the work in the fields and orchard. Benjamin and his father fished in the Patapsco River.

Benjamin loved nature and wildlife, loved learning—especially math—and showed a great interest in mechanics. At the age of twenty-two he built a striking clock entirely of wood. He played the violin and the flute. When the Ellicott brothers arrived to build their mills, the Bannekers' farm provided provisions for the workers. Benjamin and young George Ellicott shared an interest in astronomy and became friends. Ellicott lent Banneker a telescope, drafting tools, and books on astronomy. Banneker's studies made him so skilled that Major Andrew Ellicott hired him as an assistant to survey the land for the nation's new capital, Washington, D.C. Banneker made astronomical observations to determine the exact boundaries of the Federal District and maintained the regulator clock that was essential for the accuracy of the observations.

Banneker also used his expertise in astronomy to produce almanacs from 1792 to 1797. He created the chart, or ephemeris, that shows the phases of the sun, moon, and planets, the tides, and other information which we today receive from the newspaper or weather forecast. Farmers relied on almanacs and their weather predictions. One particularly useful feature of Banneker's almanacs was the prediction of Chesapeake Bay tides. Maryland's U.S. Senator James McHenry wrote the introduction to Banneker's first almanac, saying it was "fresh proof that the powers of the mind are disconnected with the colour of the skin." The almanac sold well and brought fame and income to Banneker. Banneker sent a copy to Thomas Jefferson along with a letter urging Jefferson to recognize the full humanity of blacks and to improve their conditions. He presented his almanac as evidence of the intellectual ability of people of African descent. Jefferson replied that he was so impressed he had forwarded the almanac to the Marquis de Condorcet, Secretary of the Academy of Sciences in Paris.

As Banneker aged and his health gradually declined, he decreased his farm work and also his astronomical studies. He continued to live on the farm that his father had bought until his death on October 19, 1806. Today, a park and museum stand at the site of the Banneker home.

William Henry Bishop

Physician and Activist

1849–1904

William Henry Bishop, a leading physician and community and political activist in Annapolis from 1875 to 1904, was one of the founders of the Anne Arundel County General Hospital, which opened its doors in 1902 to patients of all races. For many years, he was the only African American physician serving Anne Arundel County and Annapolis. Descended from a prominent and wealthy African American family, he became one of the most influential African Americans in the Annapolis Republican Party but never held any political office, preferring to build his medical practice. He was on the board of trustees of the area's only public school for African Americans, the Stanton Colored Public School, and a treasurer of the St. Phillip's Colored Episcopal Church.

William Henry Bishop was born in December 1849, the only child of Nicholas and Martha Wilmot Bishop, an Irish immigrant from Dublin, who died when he was three. His grandfather, William Henry Bishop, Sr. (1802–1870), himself the son of an Irish father and a slave mother, payed great attention to the upbringing of his grandson. William Senior had created a successful carting business in Annapolis, invested the profits in valuable real estate and, just prior to the Civil War, had became one of the wealthiest black residents in the city, owning seventeen houses and lots. Young William's father, Nicholas Bishop, married twice after the death of his first wife. He had four additional children, only one of whom lived to adulthood. Between 1850 and 1865, Nicholas traveled several times to the Republic of Liberia in West Africa where he owned a rubber plantation. In 1864 he also became a justice of the peace for Montserrado County in Liberia before later returning to Annapolis.

William attended Howard University's Preparatory School in Washington, D.C., from 1870 to 1872 and graduated from Howard University's medical school in 1875 as valedictorian of his class. He returned to Annapolis, moved into his grandfather's residence on Church Circle, across from St. Anne's Church, established his practice, and married Annie Elizabeth Chew of Philadelphia. They had four children: Charlotte, Martha, William, and James.

Few African Americans practiced medicine in the U.S. in the mid-1870s. At the time William Bishop graduated from medical school, only seven U.S. medical schools admitted African Americans to study. The Howard University Medical School was the only one that admitted significant numbers of African American students. The training of African Americans to be physicians faced great opposition across the U.S., even from the American Medical Association.

Bishop's first son, William, became a teacher but died in 1901 at twenty-two after a ten-month illness due to pulmonary disease. His two daughters married and remained in Annapolis. The younger son, James, also became a physician.

Dr. Bishop died on October 6, 1904, of complications from tuberculosis. The following day, the *Annapolis Evening Capitol* carried the notice of his passing on its front page and declared "Death of Dr. William Bishop, Leading Colored Citizen Passes Quietly Away." The tribute stated "Although educated, refined, and a professional man, and so light a color that he might have easily passed for a white man anywhere, Dr. Bishop was retiring, modest, and unobtrusive, always courteous and polite. . . . He was respected by the best white citizens in town and his death has removed one of the best men of his race." Bishop made an outstanding contribution to African American life in Annapolis and across Anne Arundel Country at a time when there were just a few prominent African American leaders in this region of Maryland.

James Hubert "Eubie" Blake

Jazz Composer and Musician

1883–1983

Eubie Blake was one of the most productive and enduring jazz composers as well as one of the world's greatest jazz pianists. Born in Baltimore on February 7, 1883, to former slaves John Sumner, a stevedore and Civil War veteran, and Emily Johnston, a laundress, Eubie began to show his musical talents at the age of six, when he sang and played the organ in the church he attended. When he was twelve, he sang outside saloons in a vocal quartet and received formal musical training from Llewellyn Wilson, the conductor of the Baltimore Colored Symphony. He soon went on to win a national piano contest. During his late teenage years, he was profoundly influenced by the piano playing of Jesse Pickett. In 1899, Eubie composed his first ragtime tune, the "Charleston Rag," which years later became a hit. His exceptional piano playing earned him a spot in "Dr. Frazier's Medicine Show," organized out of Fairfield, Pennsylvania, in 1901. He made his first dancing and playing appearances in New York City in 1902 but returned to Baltimore the following year to become a well-known performer at the Goldfield Hotel. Eubie moved to Atlantic City in 1905 and became a fixture there for the next nine years until 1914, when he was heard by the visiting piano great, James P. Johnson, who called him "one of the foremost pianists of all time." Eubie published his first copyrighted tune, "Chevy Chase," in 1914.

The following year, he met creative lyricist and singer Noble Sissle, and the pair agreed to go into partnership. They quickly produced their first composition, "It's All Your Fault," and soon became known as the "Dixie Duo." Sissle and Blake joined James Reese Europe in touring the United States after World War I. Their collaboration led to the production of one of the greatest black musicals of all time, "Shuffle Along," which opened in New York City on May 23, 1921. Among the memorable tunes was "I'm Just Wild about Harry," later revived by presidential candidate Harry Truman. Eubie created another massive hit in 1930 with "Memories of You," referred to by music critics as probably his best-ever pop tune. During World War II Sissle and Blake conducted their own U.S.O. show. Eubie married his first wife, Marion Grant Tyler, in 1945.

After the war, and in his sixties, Eubie enrolled in the University of New York to study music formally and graduated with a degree in 1950. He became involved in the founding of the Negro Actors Guild in response to the difficulties that African American musicians and other performers faced in the artistic and performing industry. In the late 1950s, Eubie appeared at concerts, night clubs, and special benefits, often in collaboration with Sissle. In 1959, Twentieth Century–Fox released a list of his hits entitled, "Wizard of the Ragtime Piano."

His appearance at the 1969 Newport Jazz Festival showcased his musical gifts and demonstrated that his musical talents had not diminished. Renewed interest in ragtime music in the 1970s led to a consistent demand for Eubie's music. He recorded more during this time than ever before and became one of the country's leading authorities on ragtime music. He recorded five major albums. He was now honored as an American original and in 1978 the musical "Eubie" became a great success. Three years later, in 1981, he received the Medal of Freedom from President Ronald Reagan. He made his last public appearance at the Lincoln Center in New York City on June 19, 1982, when he was ninety-nine years old. That year, his wife of thirty-six years died. Five days after his one hundredth birthday, on February 12, 1983, he died. He had become one of the most enduring American cultural personalities of the twentieth century.

George Freeman Bragg, Jr.

Episcopal Priest and Author

1863–1940

George Freeman Bragg, Jr., was one of the best-known and most highly respected black Episcopal clergymen in the nation during the first half of the twentieth century. Rector of Baltimore's St. James Episcopal Church from 1891 to 1940, he provided religious, intellectual, and social leadership within the city's black community. Bragg worked closely with Baltimore's poorest residents, yet was regarded as a friend by both Booker T. Washington and W. E. B. Du Bois as he tried to reconcile their views and visions for improving conditions for the race. Du Bois invited Bragg to be part of the launching of the Niagara Movement in 1905. Its forward-looking vision would lead to the founding of the NAACP.

Bragg was born on January 25, 1863, in Warrenton, North Carolina, to George and Mary Bragg. When he was two, his parents moved to Petersburg, Virginia, to be near his paternal grandmother, Caroline Wiley Bragg, a former slave of an Episcopal priest. George's first formal schooling was at the all-black Episcopal St. Stephen's Church School in Petersburg, where four of his uncles had pioneered the founding of the church. In 1881, at age seventeen, Bragg was appointed a page in the Virginia legislature. He soon founded a weekly newspaper, the *Lancet*. He entered an Episcopal theological school and, in 1887, was ordained a deacon. That same year he married Nellie Hill, who would be his lifelong companion. On December 19, 1888, Bragg was ordained an Episcopal priest at the St. Luke's Episcopal Church in Norfolk, Virginia. Bragg increased the modest congregation by his vision and drive and helped build a new church and rectory. At St. Luke's he founded the Industrial School for Girls and the Holy Innocents Mission.

In 1891 he was invited to become the rector of St. James Episcopal Church in Baltimore, whose congregation worshipped in rented quarters. He made the church financially independent and purchased a rectory and land on which to erect a new church building. In 1892 he founded a religious journal, the *Church Advocate,* and several years later a second paper, the *Ledger.* In 1899, he founded the Maryland Home for Friendless Colored Children and began publishing the monthly *Maryland Home*, which carried news of the children's institution. In 1912 Bragg moved the home to larger facilities on a farm near Catonsville in Baltimore County. He always encouraged the development of job skills and promoted the expansion of black educational opportunities. Bragg condemned the practice of excluding African American clergy from attending church conventions and promoted the concept of creating an African American missionary district operated under the supervision of a black bishop within the Episcopal Church.

In 1900 the *Ledger* merged with the *Afro-American* and became the *Afro-American Ledger.* Bragg was editor and John H. Murphy, Sr., was business manager. The *Afro* took strong stands in defense of black voting rights, in opposition to segregation, and in support of moral uplift. Bragg edited the newspaper until 1915. He also wrote a number of books including *The Colored Harvest of the Old Virginia Diocese* (1901), *The First Negro Priest on Southern Soil* (1909), *A Bond-Slave of Christ: Entering the Ministry Under Great Difficulties* (1912), and *The History of the Afro-American Group of the Episcopal Church* (1929). He recorded general African American history in his *Men of Maryland* (1925), *A Race with a History and a Country* (1930), and *Heroes of the Eastern Shore* (1939).

By the early 1930s, Bragg's congregation at St. James Church numbered over five hundred, and he had influenced many parishioners to follow his example into the Episcopal ministry. He died after a brief illness on March 12, 1940, and his funeral was held at the church he had served for almost fifty years.

John Edward "Grit" Bruce

Journalist

1856–1924

John Edward Bruce was one of the leading African American writers and journalists during the late nineteenth and early twentieth centuries. Well known in many social circles for his forthright approach, he produced a large volume of insightful essays reflecting the African American experience.

John started life as a slave on February 22, 1856, in primitive conditions along the Piscataway Creek in Maryland. He was the son of Robert and Martha Bruce, slaves who were forcibly separated from each other in his very early years. When John was merely three years old, his father was sold and sent to Georgia, never to be heard from by his family again. His mother's owner, Major Harvey Griffin, allowed her to work as a cook and used clothes dealer serving the soldiers at Fort Washington. During the early months of the Civil War, John and his mother marched to freedom in the company of Union soldiers, traveling north through southern Maryland into Washington, D.C., where she found and stayed with her cousin Busie Patterson. His mother worked in Washington as a domestic while John received both public and private education.

Although John enrolled in a three-month course at Howard University, he did not receive many years of formal education. Nevertheless, he read widely. Bruce was a gifted speaker and writer who became attracted to the power of the spoken and written word. He held in high esteem the writings of black nationalists and worked closely with many who supported these ideals to develop serious dialogue regarding the future of the African American community. His journalism focused on the many challenges that the African American community faced as a result of segregation and racism. He wrote regular columns for twenty black newspapers across the country and occasionally his articles appeared in white papers, including the *Boston Transcript,* the *Washington Evening Star,* the *New York Times,* the *St. Louis Globe-Democrat,* the *Buffalo Express*, and the *Sunday Republican* of Washington, D.C. He served as editor, or associate editor, of a variety of quarterlies and magazines. His writings appeared in publications originating in Africa, Europe, and the Caribbean. He wrote two books, *Short Biographical Sketches of Eminent Negro Men and Women* (1910) and *The Awakening of Hezekiah Jones* (1916) as well as hundreds of pamphlets. Like many other outstanding Marylanders of African descent, Bruce was far better known outside Maryland, because his work involved numerous interests. After working briefly for the *New York Times*, he founded his first newspaper, *Argus*, a weekly, in 1879 and afterwards established four other newspapers. Each of them, the *Sunday Item (1880),* the *Washington Grit (1884),* the *Chronicle* (1897), and the *Weekly Standard* (1908) served black subscribers in urban centers.

Bruce lived for many years in Washington, D.C., but traveled all over the U.S. and became a popular speaker. Around 1900, he moved to New York, living first in Albany and then in New York City, where he established a number of newspapers, including the *Weekly Standard* in 1908. Bruce's newspaper businesses were not financially successful, so he worked for the New York Port Authority until his retirement in 1922. He died on August 7, 1924, at the age of sixty-seven. His funeral, held at Liberty Hall in Harlem, was attended by many of the country's leading black nationalists, including Marcus Garvey. In his eulogy, Garvey acknowledged the significant role Bruce had played in the fight for human rights during the late nineteenth and early twentieth centuries. In spite of his simple beginnings and limited formal education, he became one of the most prolific and independent journalists of his time.

Cabell "Cab" Calloway, III

Musician and Composer

1907–1994

Cab Calloway sang, danced, played, composed, and recorded his way to musical fame. He was known as the "Hi-De-Ho" man, from the lyrics of his most famous song. He appeared in films and on Broadway. As leader of a well-known band, he introduced new singers and musicians to the world. One of many African American musicians who rose to prominence during the 1930s and 1940s, he made major contributions to the field of American music.

Cabell Calloway, whose father and grandfather were also named Cabell Calloway, was born in Rochester, New York, on December 25, 1907. His father was a lawyer and his mother, the former Martha Eulalia Reed, a church organist. Both were from Baltimore families, and they returned to Baltimore in 1918. For two years they lived on Druid Hill Avenue with the Calloway grandparents, who were so conservative they would not allow the children to play in the street after school. After Cab's father died, they lived with the middle-class Reeds until his mother remarried. She caught him playing dice one Sunday morning and sent him to boarding school in Pennsylvania. After a year he was ready to come home and take his studies more seriously. As a teenager, Cab sold newspapers on the street and racing forms at Pimlico racetrack. He worked with the horses, which he loved, and played baseball in Druid Hill Park. At Douglass High School, Cab played the drums, sang, and performed in vaudeville shows. W. Llewellyn Wilson, chairman of the music department at Douglass and conductor of the City Colored Orchestra, taught and encouraged the talented young musician, who also played in local clubs. Cab gave his earnings to his mother to help support the younger children. After graduation, Cab's sister Blanche, a singer, got him an audition with the director of a musical review in which she was playing at Baltimore's Royal Theater. Cab joined the show and ended up in Chicago. There, in 1928, he married Wenonah Conacher, known as "Betty." After they divorced, Cab married Zulme MacNeal. Calloway was the father of five daughters: Camay, Constance, Chris, Lael, and Cabella.

In 1928 Cab Calloway formed and led his first musical group, the Alabamians. The following year, the band opened at the Savoy Ballroom on Lenox Avenue in Harlem. At age twenty-two, Cab, leading a new band called the Missourians, worked at the famous Cotton Club, amidst the glitter of the rich and famous. In 1931, Calloway's Cotton Club Orchestra cut their first record, for which Cab wrote a theme song called "Minnie the Moocher" about a "rough, tough character with a heart of gold." In the mid-1930s the band toured Europe. At London's Palladium they played a command performance for the Prince of Wales, the future King Edward VIII. Back home, the band made several movies, including *St. Louis Blues* in 1939 and *Stormy Weather* in 1943. Lena Horne and Pearl Bailey sang with Calloway's band, which also launched the careers of jazz greats such as Dizzy Gillespie and Chuck Berry. As so often happens in show business, the group fell on hard times and had to disband in 1948.

The early 1950s brought new success as Cab played the role of "Sportin' Life" in George Gershwin's *Porgy and Bess* on Broadway and in Europe. After *Porgy*, Calloway led a small combo. In the mid-1960s, he toured with the Harlem Globetrotters. Later he played the role of Horace Vandergelder opposite Pearl Bailey in *Hello Dolly*, another Broadway hit. He published his autobiography, *Of Minnie the Moocher and Me*, in 1976. *Ebony* magazine presented Cab with its Lifetime Achievement Award in 1985. Cab Calloway died in Westchester, New York, on November 18, 1994. His talent lives on in his many recordings and films still available today.

Albert Irvin Cassell

Architectural Engineer

1895–1969

Albert Irvin Cassell was one of America's most distinguished architectural engineers of the mid-twentieth century. He was also an outstanding educator and entrepreneur for over forty years. From the 1920s to the 1960s, his productive and rewarding architectural career created outstanding buildings on the campuses of many of the nation's leading institutions of higher learning for African Americans. These included Howard University and Tuskegee Institute, as well as Morgan State University and Virginia Union University. As president of the architectural firm Cassell, Gray and Sulton, he influenced the planning and construction of large office and manufacturing buildings in industry, early apartment high-rises in public housing, and commanding church structures, as well as federal government buildings in the District of Columbia. These buildings are now valued in the millions of dollars.

Albert Irvin Cassell was born in Towson, Maryland, the third child of Charlotte Cassell and Albert Truman. Young Albert attended and completed his elementary and secondary education in Baltimore schools. He pursued his college degree, majoring in architecture at Cornell University in upstate New York. Blessed with a beautiful voice, he sang in churches to help pay for his college expenses. After the outbreak of World War I, he served in the rank of second lieutenant in the U.S. Army, in the U.S. and in France during 1917 and 1918. After the end of the war, he returned to Cornell University and graduated in 1919 with a degree in Architectural Design. His first job was as an architectural draftsman in the offices of Howard J. Wieguer of Bethlehem, Pennsylvania, where he helped design mills and industrial plants.

After less than a year, Cassell joined the faculty of Howard University in Washington, D.C., and within a few years, he became the head of Howard's Department of Architecture. Cassell worked to lay the foundation for this department and expanded its offerings so that it eventually became the College of Engineering and Architecture at Howard University.

Cassell was the leading architect in the construction of the major buildings on the campus of Howard University over a period of almost twenty years. His first major construction was the building that houses the College of Human Ecology, completed in 1921. Three years later, he would begin designing and supervising the construction of the gymnasium, armory, athletic field, three dormitories, the medical school, and the famous Freedmen's Hospital on the campus. His work transformed the campus into one of the most functional and esthetically pleasing campuses of the 1930s. Between 1929 and 1932 he supervised the university's vast maintenance department as he planned for his three most outstanding landmarks on the campus: Howard University's Chemistry Building, the Frederick Douglass Memorial Hall, and the Founder's Library, which was completed in 1938.

The elegance of his buildings on the Howard campus brought attention to his work and invitations to work on other campuses, in private enterprise, and with governmental facilities. Cassell and his engineering company were deeply involved in the planning and construction of hundreds of buildings that are today viewed as historical treasures and national landmarks.

Cassell had three wives and six children, Calvin, Charles, Martha, Alberta Jeanette, Alberta Thomas, and Paula. He died after a heart attack at his home in Washington, D.C., on November 30, 1969. He was survived by his third wife, Flora B. M. Scroggins Cassell and his children. His funeral was held at the Washington National Cathedral on December 3, 1969, and he was interred in the Baltimore National Cemetery.

Daniel Isaac Wright Coker

Minister and Teacher

1780–1846

Daniel Coker—dedicated teacher, abolitionist, colonizationist, and outspoken Methodist minister—was born in 1780 in Baltimore County, Maryland, to a slave father, Edward Wright, and white mother, Susan Coker, an indentured servant. His original name was Isaac Wright, and he grew up with white half-brothers from his mother's first marriage. Daniel accompanied his brothers to school as their valet and from this experience realized the importance of obtaining an education. Dissatisfied with life as a slave, he escaped to New York. As an adult he changed his name to Daniel after the courageous Old Testament figure and assumed his mother's surname, Coker. Having shown evidence that he was called to be a minister and greatly encouraged by the Methodist Bishop Francis Asbury, he began to preach.

Coker quietly returned to Maryland and began working to improve the free African American community in Baltimore, one of the largest in the nation. He quickly became valuable to abolitionists in Baltimore, who obtained his freedom from his former masters.

Coker taught in the African School operated by the Sharp Street Methodist Church between 1802 and 1816. He later headed the African Bethel Church School established by the African Methodist Episcopal Church community. After obtaining his freedom, Coker began to speak out against slavery and the treatment that persons of African descent experienced in the wider society as well as within the Methodist Church. On coming to the realization that the Sharp Street Methodist Church's white leaders were unwilling to change their ways, he urged African American Methodists to separate themselves from their white brethren. In 1816 he helped form the independent African Bethel Church in Baltimore. He was invited by Richard Allen to attend the Philadelphia Conference in April 1816, which sought to formally establish a national African Methodist Episcopal Church. He served as secretary of the conference and was nominated and elected the first bishop of the new A.M.E. Church, but declined the position in favor of the Church's founding clergyman, Richard Allen.

Coker emigrated to West Africa in 1820 and quickly emerged as one of the spiritual leaders of a new settlement sponsored by the American Colonization Society. The settlers suffered terribly from malaria and lack of food. The environment was so difficult that when the last of the society's agents died, Coker assumed leadership of the black American settlers. Coker took the settlers to live temporarily in the British West African colony of Sierra Leone until conditions were more favorable. When the Marylanders went to Cape Mesurado the following year, the American Colonization Society refused to reappoint Coker as the society's agent, although he was financially rewarded for his leadership during the crisis. Coker authored and published a vivid account of these critical times entitled *The Journal of Daniel Coker, A Descendant of Africa, on a Voyage for Sherbo in Africa* (1820). Coker remained in West Africa for the following twenty-six years working, preaching, and writing against slavery and the slave trade. He pastored the African Methodist Episcopal Church that he founded in Freetown, Sierra Leone, until his death in 1846. His life's work influenced and shaped the lives of countless Africans and African Americans, as he sought to bring about a more humane society on both sides of the Atlantic.

Harry Augustus Cole

Attorney and Court of Appeals Judge

1921–1999

Harry Cole was a trailblazer: the first African American state assistant attorney general, the first African American in the Maryland Senate, and the first African American judge to serve on the Maryland Court of Appeals. Known for his integrity, steadfastness, and intelligence, Judge Cole's strong commitment was to promote equal justice for all.

Harry Cole was born on New Year's Day, 1921, in Washington, D.C., the youngest of five children of Rosina Thompson Cole, a cook, and Richard Baker Cole, a tailor. His father died when Harry was a baby, and his mother brought the family to a home on McCulloh Street in Baltimore, the city where she had grown up. By age ten, Cole knew he wanted to be a lawyer. He graduated from Frederick Douglass High School in 1939, then worked for a year shining shoes and waiting tables to earn enough to begin his studies at Morgan State College, from which he graduated magna cum laude in 1943. While at Morgan, Cole helped organize a march on Annapolis to protest the state's Jim Crow laws, founded and edited the college newspaper, the *Spokesman*, and served as president of the junior class and the student council. By graduation day, he was already in the U.S. Army, training for service as an officer during World War II.

After the war, Cole studied at the University of Maryland School of Law, graduated in 1949, and became associated with the Baltimore law firm of Brown, Allen, and Watts. The following year, at age twenty-nine, he campaigned unsuccessfully for a seat in the Maryland House of Delegates and the year after that for a seat on the Baltimore City Council. In 1953, Cole was appointed a Maryland assistant attorney general. Undaunted by two political defeats, Cole, a Republican, won election to the Maryland State Senate, where he served from 1954 to 1958. By defeating a rival from Jack Pollack's powerful West Baltimore organization, Cole set an important political precedent. His victory showed that black candidates could win and stimulated other African Americans to run for public office. While in office, Cole worked with Governor Theodore McKeldin to have racial designations removed from the application forms for state jobs and opened up new job opportunities for African Americans. Defeated by a black Democrat in 1958, Cole returned to the practice of law.

Harry Cole was appointed associate judge of the Municipal Court of Baltimore City in 1967 and in 1968 associate judge of the Supreme Bench of Baltimore City. He was elected to a fifteen-year term on that bench in 1970. In 1977, he was appointed to the Maryland Court of Appeals, the highest court in the state, where he became only the fourth African American in the nation to serve on a state's highest court. Cole sat on the Court of Appeals until his retirement at age seventy in 1991. Cole remained a man of the community. A thoughtful and knowledgeable protector of a defendant's constitutional rights, he demanded excellence of young lawyers and freely dissented when he disagreed with the court's majority.

Harry Cole married Doris Freeland Cole in 1957. They had three daughters: Susan, Harriette, and Stephanie. After his retirement, Cole chaired the Baltimore City Charter Revision Commission and, in 1995, became chair of the Morgan State University Board of Regents. At Morgan, Cole's first commitment was to the students and their welfare. The Honorable Harry Cole served on numerous boards throughout his life, including those of the Baltimore Museum of Art, the Baltimore Zoological Society, the Union Memorial Hospital, the Baltimore City and Maryland Bar Associations, and the National Association for the Advancement of Colored People. He died in Baltimore on February 14, 1999.

Silas Edwin Craft

Educator and Activist

1918–1995

Born on June 5, 1918, in Chatham, Virginia, the third of six children of Silas Birdsong Craft and Ada Rebecca Graves Craft, Silas Craft spent his formative years in Gary, West Virginia, under the direct supervision of his maternal grandfather, Reverend Stephen Thomas Graves, who encouraged him to obtain a formal education. Unable to pay public school fees, young Craft worked as a coal miner at the Koppers Coal Company in Kimball, West Virginia, to help pay for his education. He excelled, graduating from Kimball High School and Bluefield State College with a degree in mathematics in 1944. A year earlier he married his college sweetheart, Dorothye Beatryce McKnight of Bluefield. Soon after graduating he trained as a civilian cadet at the Tuskegee Air Base in Alabama.

In August 1944, Craft responded to an invitation to work in Howard County, Maryland, where there were few professionally trained African Americans. He was appointed principal of the Cooksville Colored School, the only black junior high school in the county, with students from the townships of Daisy, Clarksville, Dayton, Glenelg, Ellicott City, and Atholton. The county supplied two buses—not an easy trip for everyone—but Craft worked hard to make the academic experience worthwhile. He helped establish the county's first senior high school for African Americans, the Harriet Tubman High School in Simpsonville. He became its first principal and held the position for seven years. After the Supreme Court's *Brown* decision in 1954, Howard County slowly began to desegregate its schools and he was involved in implementation of that process.

In 1956 Craft accepted the principalship of Montgomery County's all-black Carver High School in Rockville. He then became assistant principal of Montgomery Blair High School (1960–65) and Francis Scott Key Junior High (1967–71), and principal of Kensington Junior High School (1971–74). He taught at Richard Montgomery High School, and worked at the Montgomery County Education Department until his retirement in 1976.

Craft also worked outside Maryland to aid the transition to desegregated schools. In 1966 he took academic leave and served as Director of Community Service Schools for the Mid-Continent Regional Educational Laboratory in Kansas City, Missouri. He was a consultant for the University of Missouri at Kansas City on desegregation matters and for a series of desegregation workshops for the state principals in Oklahoma. His formal training included a master of science degree from the University of Pennsylvania, graduate work at Harvard, and work on a doctoral degree that he did not complete at the University of Maryland. Two years after his retirement, Bluefield bestowed on him an honorary doctorate, and in his later years he was always addressed as Dr. Craft.

After his retirement Craft was one of the leading members of the First Baptist Church of Guilford, an early and active black congregation in Howard County, founded in 1901. He was chairperson of the church's board of trustees for more than a decade. He served on the executive board of the Howard County branch of the NAACP and on the organization's national board of directors. He coauthored *History of Blacks in Howard County, Maryland* (1986) and helped establish the Howard County Center for African American Culture in 1987.

Craft and his wife raised six children. On January 12, 1995, he died at home in Columbia, Maryland, having left a rich legacy of community service. His obituary observed, "He never accepted second best. For him, only the best would do."

Harry Sythe Cummings

Politician, Lawyer, and Businessman

1866–1917

Harry Cummings was the first African American to hold public office in Baltimore City, serving numerous terms on the City Council from his election in 1890 until his death in 1917. Active in national Republican politics, he stumped the country at election time to urge blacks to vote for the party of Reconstruction. One of a growing number of black professionals in the late nineteenth century, Cummings practiced law and operated a real estate business in Baltimore. He sought to improve life for African Americans while at the same time fighting off attempts by some to undo the progress made during and after the Civil War.

Harry Sythe Cummings was born in Baltimore on May 19, 1866, to the former Eliza Jane Davage, who ran a boarding house and sometimes worked in domestic service, and Henry Cummings, hotel chef. Harry's sister Ida became well-known in the fields of education and women's organizations. Grandparents on both sides were born slaves in Baltimore County. Harry Cummings married the former Blanche Conklin and had four children, of whom two, Harry, Jr. and Louise, lived to adulthood. Cummings attended the Baltimore Colored High School, later Frederick Douglass High School, and graduated from Lincoln University in Pennsylvania in 1886. He became one of the first two African American students admitted to the University of Maryland Law Department in 1887, completed the three-year program in two years, and graduated in 1889. He was admitted to the Maryland Bar and credentialed to practice law before the Maryland Court of Appeals and the United States District Court. In 1890 he won election to the Baltimore City Council from the racially mixed Republican Eleventh Ward in West Baltimore. From then until his death in 1917, West Baltimore almost always had black representation by Cummings, Dr. John Marcus Cargill, or Hiram Watty.

At the time, few African Americans held public office across the nation. The former Confederate states had disenfranchised blacks, and most northern states had small black populations. A handful of border states had sizable black populations and black suffrage. In Maryland, Baltimore, Annapolis, and Cambridge all elected black city councilmen. These men fought an uphill battle, working hard for each small gain as they struggled to prevent serious losses. With help from immigrant Democrats, Cummings and his colleagues defeated numerous attempts to disenfranchise Maryland African Americans. Cummings fought against housing segregation laws that were finally declared unconstitutional by the United States Supreme Court, and convinced the council to open a Manual Training School for black students. He convinced the council to appoint music and art teachers for the city's black schools and authored legislation establishing a kindergarten in all public schools, black and white.

Cummings extended councilmanic courtesies to African Americans. His resolution to invite the National Negro Business League to hold its 1908 convention in Baltimore was approved. Booker T. Washington, who financially supported Cummings' campaigns, presided over some of the meetings. At the 1904 Republican Party convention in Chicago, Cummings gave a rousing speech seconding the nomination of Theodore Roosevelt. Several months later, he and two other black Marylanders were invited to the White House. When World War I approached, Cummings urged the inclusion of African Americans in the armed forces, noting the historic patriotism of blacks in earlier wars. Harry Cummings, one of a remarkable generation of African American pioneers in politics and the professions, died in Baltimore on September 6, 1917.

Ida Rebecca Cummings

Teacher and Volunteer

1867–1958

Ida Rebecca Cummings was born in Baltimore on March 17, 1867, one of six children of Eliza Jane Davage Cummings and Henry Cummings. Her father worked as a chef and owned a catering business. Her mother operated a boarding house. Her brother, Harry, was the first African American to serve on the Baltimore City Council. Her grandparents had been slaves in Baltimore County. Ida was educated in the city's public schools and by the Oblate Sisters of Providence, at Hampton Institute, and at Morgan College. She also studied at Columbia University, at the Kindergarten Training School in Baltimore, and at the Chicago Kindergarten College. Ida learned her activism by example. When Ida was a girl, she often accompanied her mother soliciting funds for Morgan College. Ida's aunt, Charlotte Davage, served as president of the Colored Young Women's Christian Association.

Ida Cummings was one of the first kindergarten teachers in Baltimore. The important field of early childhood education was new in the first years of the twentieth century, and Cummings understood how important the early years were for children's future success. She convinced her brother to introduce an ordinance that established kindergartens in all the public schools of Baltimore, for both black and white children. In 1904, Ida and Eliza Cummings, along with several other Baltimore women, established the Colored Empty Stocking and Fresh Air Circle. Ida served as president for many of its forty years. At Christmas time, the women filled stockings with candies and toys. In the summer they raised money for city children to spend a week in the country, initially boarding with rural families. In 1906 the Circle offered a free excursion to Brown's Grove, a Chesapeake Bay beach. In 1907 the organization bought a farm at Delight, on the route of the Emory Grove Trolley Line, with ten and a half acres that had "fruit and shade trees, outhouses, and good water." The women of the Circle paid $750 in cash and borrowed another $1,000 to pay for the farm, then organized committees to solicit furniture, bedding, and other needs. This work, which benefited thousands of children over the years, was accomplished before national or local governments played a significant role in developing social programs. Without women's organizations, much would have been left undone.

In addition to her work with children, Ida Cummings was active in numerous women's organizations. She was a member of the National Association of Colored Women. She served as corresponding secretary from 1912 to 1914, and as treasurer from 1914 to 1916. Cummings arranged to have the biennial meeting held at Bethel African Methodist Episcopal Church in Baltimore in 1916, and was then elected vice-president-at-large of this major national organization. She organized campaigns for women's suffrage and against lynching. After women won the vote in 1920 by amendment to the United States Constitution, Cummings and others conducted voter registration campaigns in Baltimore to sign up both women and men from the African American community. She served as president of the Women's Republican League.

Cummings founded the Frances Ellen Watkins Harper Temple of Elks and held the office of daughter ruler. She served as director for the Maryland Elks Department of Education and national chair of the Child Welfare Department. Cummings worked with the YWCA and was a member of the board of the Cheltenham School for Boys. An active supporter of Morgan College, she became the first woman trustee in 1919. When Ida Cummings died in Baltimore on November 8, 1958, she still lived in her family house at 1234 Druid Hill Avenue in the city to which she had given so much during her ninety years of life.

Leon Day

Baseball Player

1916–1995

Leon Day, elected to the Baseball Hall of Fame in 1995, was an ace pitcher in baseball's National Negro League during the 1930s and 1940s. His versatility made him especially valuable. The 5-ft. 9-in. hard-throwing right-hander frequently hit over .300 and could play both infield and outfield positions when needed. A modest man, he was known for his sense of humor. Leon Day was a true athlete of the old style, devoted to and excelling in his sport in the days before professional athletes earned big money.

Leon Day was born on October 30, 1916, in Alexandria, Virginia. He was still a baby when his family moved to Baltimore. He played sandlot baseball in Mt. Winans in south Baltimore and sneaked into Maryland Park in nearby Westport to watch the Baltimore Black Sox of the Eastern Colored League and his childhood hero, pitcher Laymon Yokely. Day attended Frederick Douglass High School. In 1934, when he was seventeen, he left school to join the Black Sox. Day earned $60 a month that season. At the peak of his highly acclaimed career, he never earned more than $350 a month.

In 1935, Day moved to the Brooklyn Eagles. He pitched the opening day game his rookie year in the National Negro League, led the Eagles' pitching staff in games won, and pitched in the All-Star East-West Classic, the first of his many appearances in that contest. He was named 1935 Rookie of the Year. The following season, the Eagles were sold and moved to Newark, New Jersey, where Day played for most of his career. In 1937, he went 13–0 and batted .320 with eight home runs. The following year, an arm injury kept him from pitching. Hard work and determination brought him back for a winning season in 1939. In 1942 he pitched a record game with 18 strikeouts against the Baltimore Elite Giants. In 1942 and 1943 he was named to the *Pittsburgh Courier's* All-American Team for the Negro Leagues.

Leon Day was drafted into the U.S. Army in 1943 to fight in World War II. He served in the 818th Amphibious Battalion, which landed on Utah Beach in Normandy, France. In 1946, Leon Day returned to the Newark Eagles in time to pitch the only opening day no-hitter ever in Negro League history, against the Philadelphia Stars. That year, he led the league in strikeouts and innings pitched while batting well over .300. Like many North American players, Leon Day spent winters in Latin America, playing baseball in Puerto Rico, Cuba, and Venezuela. He played two seasons with the Mexico City Reds before returning to the United States.

In 1949, Leon Day came home to Baltimore and helped the Baltimore Elite Giants win the pennant. He began the 1950 season with the Elite Giants and then moved to an integrated minor league team in Winnipeg, Canada. He played with the International League Toronto Maple Leafs, the Eastern League Scranton Miners, and several other teams before retiring in 1954. Never a rich man, Day worked after his retirement as a security guard, as a mail carrier, and as a bartender in the lounge of former teammate Lennie Pearson.

Leon Day's final years were spent with his wife Geraldine in Baltimore. He received, albeit belatedly, a number of awards to honor his stunning career. In 1973 Day was inducted into the Newark Baseball Hall of Fame and in 1993 into the Puerto Rico Baseball Hall of Fame. He was honored at the White House by President George Bush in 1992 and by Vice-President Al Gore in 1994. A park along the Gwynn's Falls in west Baltimore has been named in his honor. Leon Day became the twelfth Negro League player to be elected to the Baseball Hall of Fame in Cooperstown, New York, shortly before his death on March 13, 1995.

Frederick Douglass

Abolitionist and Statesman

CA. 1818–1895

Frederick Douglass led the African American struggle to abolish slavery and establish equal rights for all. His brilliant orations drew crowds in the United States and abroad, and his weekly newspapers and three autobiographies were read widely by blacks and whites alike.

Douglass was born Frederick Augustus Washington Bailey in February 1817 or 1818 in Talbot County, Maryland. His mother, Harriet Bailey, was a slave whose family had lived on the Eastern Shore for generations. He never knew his father. At age seven, Frederick was sent to the residence of his master. Harriet walked the twelve miles to visit him for the last time in February 1825. She died soon afterward. In 1826 he was sent to Fells Point in Baltimore, where he enjoyed the relative freedom of city life and learned to read and write. With his first cash he bought a book. Later in life he wrote, "Education . . . means emancipation; it means light and liberty."

As a teenager, Frederick worked at a shipyard. His pay went to his master. In 1833 he was sent to St. Michaels in Talbot County and turned over to a "slavebreaker" who tried to beat Frederick into submission, but Douglass fought back and the beatings stopped. Douglass returned to Baltimore and worked as a caulker at a shipyard in Fells Point where he was beaten by whites who feared competition from black workers. In 1838 he escaped, by train, to New York City. He married Anna Murray, a free black woman from Maryland. The couple moved to New Bedford, Massachusetts, where Frederick took the surname Douglass. Frederick and Anna had five children: Rosetta, Lewis, Frederick, Charles, and Annie.

In 1839, Douglass became a paid lecturer for the Massachusetts Anti-Slavery Society. He stirred crowds with accounts of the horrors of slavery. In 1845 he published *The Narrative of the Life of Frederick Douglass* and then left for a speaking tour of Britain to avoid being captured and returned to slavery. British friends raised $700 to pay for his freedom. In 1847 he returned home, settled in Rochester, New York, and began publishing an antislavery weekly, the *North Star,* called *Frederick Douglass' Paper* after 1851. He assisted slaves escaping to Canada. He opposed the colonization of free blacks "back" to Africa, proclaiming that African Americans had a right to freedom and prosperity in the land of their birth. He gave a keynote speech at the first Women's Rights Convention in Seneca Falls, New York, in 1848 and supported women's suffrage. Douglass, who lived in a state where propertied black men could vote, believed that political action and interracial coalitions were valuable weapons in the struggle for equality and campaigned actively for the Republican Party. He also taught self-reliance saying, "If we succeed in the race of life, it must be by our own energies, and our own exertions."

When the Civil War broke out, Douglass urged President Lincoln to enlist black soldiers and argued that people who paid taxes and fought in the military merited the right to vote. After the war, he received several appointments from Republican administrations: president of the Freedmen's Bank, and marshal and recorder of deeds for the District of Columbia.

Douglass bought a twenty-room house overlooking the Anacostia River. "Cedar Hill" is now a museum. In 1881 he published *The Life and Times of Frederick Douglass.* After Anna died, Douglass married Helen Pitts, his former secretary. The fact that she was white caused some controversy. In 1888 Douglass was named Minister-Resident and Consul-General to the Republic of Haiti and Charge d'Affaires to Santo Domingo. In 1891, Frederick and Helen retired to Cedar Hill. On February 20, 1895, Douglass, considered by many the most prominent African American of the nineteenth century, died at home. He was buried in Rochester, New York.

Christian Abraham Fleetwood

Civil War Soldier and Civil Servant

1840–1914

Christian Fleetwood was awarded the highest military honor for his bravery in action in Virginia during the Civil War. He was one of over 200,000 African Americans who joined the United States Colored Troops and the U.S. Navy to fight for the Union and for an end to slavery. He was one of more than twenty African Americans awarded the Congressional Medal of Honor for their heroism during the Civil War.

Christian Abraham Fleetwood was born in Baltimore on July 21, 1840, the son of Charles and Ann Maria Fleetwood, free people of color. His father worked as the chief steward in the household of a Baltimore merchant, John Brune. When young Christian was only four or five, Mrs. Brune, who was childless, began to teach him reading, writing, and figuring. The young man used the Brunes' library and acquired an education. Although it was not illegal in Maryland, as it was in most southern states, education for young blacks was not encouraged. There were no public schools for black students until after 1870. At sixteen, Fleetwood went to work in the office of the Maryland Colonization Society, an organization that established a colony in Liberia as a haven for former slaves. Fleetwood learned business and bookkeeping, planning to go later to Liberia as an agent for the Brune mercantile concern. When he was still sixteen, Fleetwood made a voyage to West Africa where he visited both Liberia and Sierra Leone. Upon his return to the United States, Fleetwood enrolled at Ashmun Institute, now Lincoln University, in Chester County, Pennsylvania. He took a business course, studying bookkeeping, math, English, grammar, geography, history, philosophy, Spanish, and French. He graduated in 1860, returned to Baltimore, and took a job in the office of merchants trading with England and Liberia. From 1860 until 1863, Fleetwood, along with several friends, published the *Lyceum Observer*, a newspaper of the Galbraith Lyceum, a local African American literary society.

In August 1863, Fleetwood enlisted in the 4th Regiment, United States Colored Troops. Because of his education and leadership ability, he was quickly promoted to sergeant-major, the highest rank an enlisted man could attain. The 4th Regiment U.S.C.T. saw action in Virginia and North Carolina. In a brutal battle before Petersburg, Virginia, Fleetwood saved many lives. At New Market Heights, part of the larger battle of Chaffin's Farm, Virginia, on September 29, 1864, Fleetwood seized the national colors after two color-bearers had been shot down and carried them through the fight, an act so courageous that he won the Congressional Medal of Honor. A vacancy opened among the regiment's all-white officers, who supported Fleetwood's nomination to fill it, but Secretary of War Edwin M. Stanton denied the promotion because of Fleetwood's race. On May 10, 1866, he received an honorable discharge in Baltimore.

After the war, Fleetwood lived in Washington, D.C., where he married Sara Iredell, a nurse, in November 1869. He received appointments to various government jobs: as a bookkeeper and teller at the Freedmen's Bank; for the government of the District of Columbia; and, from 1881 to 1914, as a clerk at the War Department. Fleetwood joined the Washington Cadet Corps, later part of the National Guard. In 1887, President Grover Cleveland commissioned him a National Guard major. Fleetwood helped organize the Colored High School Cadet Corps in Washington. Christian Fleetwood died on September 28, 1914, in Washington, D.C. A chapel at the District of Columbia National Guard Armory is named for him. His Medal of Honor was put on display at the Armed Forces Hall of the Smithsonian Institution's National Museum of American History.

Edward Franklin Frazier

Sociologist

1894–1962

Edward Frazier was one of America's leading sociologists of the mid-twentieth century. His pioneering study, *The Negro Family in the United States* (1939), presented the first constructive sociological analysis of the plight of the African American family, changing forever the negative and biased thinking that pervaded most sociological literature. During his almost thirty-year professional career as researcher, educator, and sociologist, Frazier distinguished himself with his views and writings on the major challenges facing the African American family between the Great Depression and the early Civil Rights period. His first books, *The Negro Family in Chicago* and *The Free Negro Family*, were both published in 1932.

Edward Franklin Frazier was born in Baltimore, Maryland, on September 24, 1894, one of five children of James Edward Frazier, a bank messenger, and Mary E. Hattie (Clark) Frazier, neither of whom had any formal education. Despite very humble beginnings, he was an excellent student, graduating from the Baltimore Colored High School in 1912. He graduated with honors from Howard University in 1916, received a master's degree in sociology from Clark University in 1920, and earned a doctorate from the University of Chicago in 1931. Numerous awards and honors for his work included a Guggenheim Research Grant, and in 1948 he became president of the American Sociological Association, the first person of African descent to lead a major American scholarly organization. Between 1951 and 1953 he also served as chief of the Division of Applied Social Sciences of the United Nations Educational Scientific and Cultural Organization (UNESCO) in Paris. He lectured on campuses across the U.S. and in Europe and held various appointments at major universities but remained head of the sociology department at Howard University until 1960.

Frazier's classic work, *The Negro Family in the United States*, won the 1939 Anisfield Award for the book that had made the most significant contribution of any work that year to the study of race relations in the United States. Frazier's second major publication, *The Black Bourgeoisie*, was written in French and published in Paris during 1955. The American edition did not appear until 1957. The thesis, which examined the development of the African American middle class emerging out of the background of American slavery and the rigid segregation system that replaced it, was far more controversial. Reviews in the leading sociological journals attacked his methodology and conclusions. Another major work was *Race and Culture Contacts in the Modern World* (1957). His last book, *The Negro Church in America* (1963), was published posthumously by the University of Liverpool.

Frazier served in leadership roles in many professional sociology organizations. He was also president of the District of Columbia Sociological Society from 1943 to 1944, the Eastern Sociological Society from 1944 to 1945, and the American Sociological Association from 1948 to 1949. He lectured at many of America's leading universities as well as the Universities of London, Edinburgh, and Liverpool. He received honorary doctorates from Morgan State University in 1955 and the University of Edinburgh in 1960. He died on May 17, 1962, in Washington, D.C., and was survived by his wife, Marie Brown Frazier, after forty years of marriage.

Joseph "Baby Joe" Gans

Boxing Champion

1874–1910

Baby Joe" Gans was a pioneering boxing champion in the United States. Experts and practitioners referred to this 133-pound, 5 ft. 6 in. handsome African-American as "the King of them all" and "the Old Master." He was lightweight champion between 1901 and 1908 but would face opponents at any weight permissible.

On May 12, 1901, Gans won the lightweight championship at Fort Erie, Ontario, Canada, by first round knockout. In the next seven years, he fought and won matches with the best light- and middle-weight boxers. His greatest bout was a victory against "Battling" Nelson in 1906 at the Goldfield in Nevada that lasted forty-two rounds. The following year he opened the three-story "Goldfield Hotel" at the corner of East Lexington and Colvin Streets in downtown Baltimore with part of the $11,000 prize money he had received, naming it after the tiny Nevada mining town where he had won his most celebrated match.

Joseph Saifuss Butts, born in Baltimore on November 25, 1874, was named after his father, a well-known Negro baseball player. When he was four years old, he was adopted by Maria Gant, who also gave him her name. Early in his boxing career, writers began to call him "Gans," and he never corrected them.

Gans attended school in East Baltimore and first worked in the city's public markets. His first "professional" fight—a victory—took place at the Avon Club in 1890, when he was a teenager. He won his second fight at Baltimore's Monumental Theater. Soon afterward, he acquired a local manager, Al Hatford. Gans's clean-cut appearance, unusual agility, and extraordinary power made him a hometown favorite. In an age of heightened racial tension, segregation, and lynching, white managers frequently took advantage of black boxers. Gans fought most of his opponents in Baltimore. His purses reached $11,000, and he used much of his prize money to help his mother and the rest of his family. In addition to the hotel, he ran a gymnasium and popular saloon. His guests included popular boxing stars of the time, from John L. Sullivan to Jack Johnson. Eubie Blake, who entertained guests at the Goldfield, remarked, "Gans did things in a big way . . . he spent his money." Blake also recalled that Gans was "the first African American in Baltimore to own an automobile."

Gans's most widely publicized fight was a rematch with Nelson on July 4, 1908, before a crowd of about 10,000 in an open-air arena near San Francisco. Gans was knocked out in the seventeenth round. His fans believed that he had been defeated by declining health. Gallant attempts were made to help him with a series of treatments and a stint at a clinic in Arizona. In the summer of 1910, his health rapidly failing, he returned to Baltimore as a hero. Carried by stretcher and ambulance to his mother's residence, Gans spent his last few days with his wife Margaret and relatives. According to some, he came to believe in Father Divine, who lived in Baltimore but who was not yet the well-known religious cult figure he would later become.

Gans died of tuberculosis on August 11, 1910, and received a hero's burial. Thousands of Baltimoreans paid respects to one of the city's outstanding black sports figures. The funeral service was held at the Whatcoat Methodist Episcopal Church at Pine and Franklin Streets. His coffin was taken to the Mount Auburn Cemetery in Westport, accompanied by three large wagons of flowers and hundreds of fans. Among the staunchest was H. L. Mencken, who lobbied in his newspaper columns for a civic monument in the fighter's memory. In 1973, "Baby" Joe became the first African American sports figure to be inducted into the Maryland Athletic Hall of Fame.

Henry Highland Garnet

Clergyman and Abolitionist

1815–1882

Henry Highland Garnet was born a slave on a New Market plantation in Kent County, on the Eastern Shore of Maryland on December 23, 1815. His family's oral tradition held that in Africa his grandfather was a Mandingo chief. At the age of nine, he escaped with his parents and settled in New York City. His father, George, worked as a shoemaker and enrolled him in New York's African Free School No. 1, but the family was forced to relocate to Long Island where his father worked as an indentured servant for two years. Henry injured his right leg, and complications forced an amputation. Determined to resume his education, he attended the Noyes Academy in New Canaan, New Hampshire, which was destroyed the next year by neighbors, who disliked having a neighborhood integrated school. He helped save some of his fellow students amid the violence and, undaunted, enrolled in 1836 at the Oneida Theological Institute at Whiteshore, near Utica, New York. Four years later, Garnet graduated at the head of his class and began teaching in Troy, New York. In 1842 he became an ordained minister and was installed as the pastor of the Liberty Street Presbyterian Church in Troy. In Troy he also became involved in the Underground Railroad and edited the *Clarion* and other black newspapers.

Garnet's major contribution to the abolitionist struggle was his successful attempt to revive the Negro Convention movement. At the August 1843 Buffalo convention, he passionately scolded the delegates, pointing out that it was their religious duty to resist slavery. He dramatically called for all American slaves to revolt against their masters. Many scholars believe that his speech signaled a major turning point in the struggle to end slavery. His appeal was published and widely distributed and became the central issue discussed within the American Antislavery Society for years. Along with Frederick Douglass, he became actively involved in the founding of the Liberty Party that would eventually become the Republican Party, and he also championed the causes of temperance and mass education.

After the passage of the Fugitive Slave Act of 1850, Garnet was invited to undertake an extensive speaking tour of Western Europe. He spent three busy years speaking to audiences in Britain, France, and Germany, where he lectured in the language of the country, greatly impressing his listeners. He also served for a brief period as a missionary in Jamaica before returning to the U.S. in 1855 to pastor the Shiloh Presbyterian Church in New York City. In 1858 he was elected president of the African Civilization Society, working to improve the image of Africa and Africans in America as well as promoting many African American self-help projects.

After the outbreak of the Civil War, Garnet was one of the first African Americans to call on President Abraham Lincoln to authorize the enlistment of African American troops. Toward the end of the war, Garnet moved to Washington to become the pastor of the Fifteenth Street Presbyterian Church. His impassioned sermons led to an invitation to preach before the House of Representatives in 1865. After the war ended, Garnet served briefly with the Freedmen's Bureau before moving back to New York City.

By then in his sixties and in declining health, Garnet continued to push for the ideas he had held since his youth. President James A. Garfield appointed him ambassador to Liberia in 1881. Garnet was honored by a gala dinner in January 1882 on his arrival in Monrovia. Within weeks, on February 12, 1882, Garnet died. He received a state funeral and was buried in Monrovia's only cemetery, overlooking the Atlantic Ocean.

Frances Ellen Watkins Harper

Poet and Lecturer

1825–1911

Frances Ellen Watkins was born to free parents in Baltimore in 1825. She was orphaned when very young and raised by an aunt and uncle who were active in the antislavery movement. Her uncle, William Watkins, ran a private school for free black students. Frances attended Watkins' Academy until she was in her early teens when she went to work as a housekeeper for a family who owned a bookstore. She read widely and began writing poetry and essays.

In 1850 Watkins moved to Ohio, where she taught domestic science at Union Seminary, an African Methodist Episcopal Church school that later became part of Wilberforce University. The next year she published her first book of prose and poetry, *Forest Leaves,* sometimes printed as *Autumn Leaves*. In 1852 she moved to Little York, Pennsylvania, where she taught school. In 1853 Maryland passed a law prohibiting free blacks from entering the state. This meant that Frances Watkins could not go home. She moved to Philadelphia where she lived at a station on the Underground Railroad. She became a paid speaker for the Maine Anti-Slavery Society and then for the larger Pennsylvania Anti-Slavery Society. Traveling widely, sometimes lecturing several times in one day, she was known for sharing her earnings with people in need. In 1854 she produced her second book, *Poems on Miscellaneous Subjects*, with a preface by abolitionist William Lloyd Garrison. It sold over 50,000 copies in the next twenty years. One frequently reprinted antislavery poem is "Bury Me in a Free Land." It concludes:

> *I ask no monument, proud and high*
> *To arrest the gaze of passers-by;*
> *All that my yearning spirit craves,*
> *Is bury me not in the land of slaves.*

In 1860 Frances Watkins married a young widower, M. Fenton Harper. They purchased a farm near Cincinnati and had one daughter, Mary. After her husband died in 1864, Frances resumed her lecturing, taking Mary with her when she traveled. She lectured on the problems faced by newly freed African Americans in the South, on the need for reform, on women's issues, and on the evils of liquor. From 1875 to 1882 she served as superintendent of the "colored branch" of the Philadelphia and Pennsylvania chapters of the Women's Christian Temperance Union and from 1883 to 1890 as director of the Northern United States Temperance Union. She was active in the National Council of Women, the American Women's Suffrage Association, and the American Association for Education of Colored Youth. She helped organize the National Association of Colored Women and served as its vice-president.

Throughout the postwar years of lecturing and activism, Frances Harper continued to write. In 1869 she published a long narrative poem, *Moses: A Story of the Nile*. This was followed by *Sketches of Southern Life* (1872), *Atlanta Offering* (1895), *Poems* (1900), and *Idylls of the Bible* (1901.) She published one novel, *Iola Leroy; or Shadows Uplifted* in 1892. The novel was set during Reconstruction, a time of widespread poverty among former slaves, discriminatory Black Codes, and racial tension. Typically Victorian, the novel aims to teach lessons to readers. The heroine, Iola, who could have passed as white, chooses to be a part of the black community. She is committed to social uplift and believes that every woman should be able to support herself, a strong feminist position. Eventually she marries an African American physician who shares her philosophy. Frances Ellen Watkins Harper died in Philadelphia on February 20, 1911.

Josiah Henson
Abolitionist and Businessman
1789–1883

Henson was one of six children born to a slave family on a Charles County farm. After his father was sold to an Alabama planter, never to return, his mother's owner, Dr. Josiah McPherson, gave the child his own first name and his uncle's surname, Henson. From his childhood, Josiah worked hard for his masters and encouraged other slaves to do the same. On Isaac Riley's plantation in Montgomery County, he was made slave "manager." On another occasion, Henson was severely beaten for protecting his drunken master. His master even entrusted Henson with taking a group of slaves to his brother's plantation in Davies County, Kentucky. Despite efforts by African Americans in Cincinnati to persuade Henson to free the slaves in his care, all arrived in Kentucky. There Henson would work as "superintendent" of slaves for three years. He once had the opportunity to kill his new master but did not. "What!" He asked himself. "Commit murder and you a Christian?" Henson began to preach as a Methodist Episcopal minister, and married. He became convinced that the institution of slavery was evil and would later write that slavery made slaves "the cringing, treacherous, false, and thieving victims of tyranny."

In October 1830, Henson fled with his wife and four of his children, following the Underground Railroad through Buffalo, New York, to Canada. He twice reentered the U.S. and led slaves from Kentucky to Canada. He became a leader in his African American community, serving as a captain in the second Essex Company of Colored Volunteers, and defended his new homeland at Fort Malden in 1837–38. In 1842 he co-founded the British-American Manual Labor Institute in Dawn, Canada, a training school for African American immigrants. He also established a business exporting Canadian walnut lumber products to Boston. Henson entered his lumber in London's "Crystal Palace Exhibition" and won a bronze medal. During that trip he became a celebrity to Britain's upper classes and was invited to meet some of Britain's leading statesmen, including Prime Minister Lord John Russell and the Archbishop of Canterbury.

On returning to the U.S., Henson's renown, and the publication in 1849 of his autobiography, *The Life of Josiah Henson, Formerly a Slave, Now an Inhabitant of Canada, as Narrated by Himself*, attracted the attention of Harriet Beecher Stowe, who was writing a novel to reveal the cruelty of American slavery. Early in 1850, while visiting her brother in Boston, she was introduced to Henson, who was in the city on business, and decided to use his experiences in her work. She had been to the places Henson had described and had lived in Cincinnati. *Uncle Tom's Cabin,* whose title character was based on Henson's experiences, sold 300,000 copies and contributed to the tension that led to the Civil War. It also gave the English language the term "Uncle Tom," which today refers to a someone docile, submissive, and eager to follow authority, although Stowe's Uncle Time did eventually turn against slavery.

A larger edition of his autobiography entitled *Truth, Stranger than Fiction: Father Henson's Story of His Own Life,* with an introduction by Stowe, appeared in 1858. In 1878 publication of a British version, *An Autobiography of Josiah Henson, (Mrs. Harriet Beecher Stowe's "Uncle Tom"),* coincided with a second trip to Europe, during which Henson met Queen Victoria at Windsor Castle. Later, President Rutherford B. Hayes greeted him at the White House. Henson died in Dresden, Canada, on May 5, 1883, at the age of ninety-four. For fifty-three years as a free man, he had fought for the dignity of African Americans, recalling that as a teenager he had first heard about becoming free from a white abolitionist. "From my earliest recollection," he wrote, "freedom had been the object of my ambition."

Matthew Alexander Henson

Explorer

1866–1955

Matthew Henson, a man who loved adventure, traveled many times to the Arctic in the late nineteenth and early twentieth centuries. He was one of the small number of explorers who became true Arctic experts.

Matthew Alexander Henson was born on August 8, 1866, on his parents' farm in Charles County. His father was a freeborn sharecropper. When Matthew was four, his family moved to Georgetown, outside Washington, D.C. Matthew's mother died when he was seven, and his father soon thereafter. Matthew lived with an uncle and attended black public schools. At thirteen he went to work as a waiter and dishwasher in a restaurant, sleeping in the kitchen and eating leftover food. His interest in travel may have been kindled when he met a sailor from Baltimore.

In 1879, Henson walked from Washington to the docks of Baltimore where he talked himself into a job on a ship departing for China, Japan, Africa, France, and the Russian Arctic. Encouraged by the ship's captain, Henson studied the history and geography of the places they visited and learned sailing skills such as carpentry, ship's mechanics, and first aid. After Captain Childs died in 1883, Henson left the ship and worked at a variety of jobs. While working at Steinmetz's hat store in Washington, D.C., he met a customer, Lieutenant Robert Peary, U.S. Navy. Peary offered Matthew a job as his personal servant during an upcoming voyage to Nicaragua and in 1887, they set out to look for a route to build a canal through Central America. Henson took over as chief surveyor when the first man quit after being stuck in quicksand. When the voyage to Nicaragua was ending, Peary asked Henson if he would like to sail to the Arctic.

The destination in 1891 was Greenland. There, Henson quickly befriended the local Inuit, who taught him the language along with hunting and tracking skills. Henson soon became an expert dogsled driver. On the second trip to Greenland in 1893, one of Henson's Inuit friends led the party to some meteorites, an extremely valuable find. Subsequent expeditions attempted to reach the North Pole, a feat that had not yet been achieved. At certain times of the year the Arctic sun never rises, and it is bitterly cold all the time. On the trip to complete mapping the north coast of Greenland, they determined that there was no land route to the North Pole. It was on this trip that Henson saved Peary's life when the captain was frostbitten and suffering with gangrene. Peary lost most of his toes and had great difficulty traveling; Henson often led the way. Several subsequent attempts to reach the North Pole failed. In 1908 and 1909, they made one last trip. Peary claimed to have reached their goal but did not show Henson the sextant, which would have identified the exact geographical location of the North Pole. Thus Henson never saw the confirming data. Others would challenge Peary's claim to have been the first to reach the true North Pole. Probably, Peary and Henson came close, with Henson in the lead.

Between journeys, Henson had lectured on the Arctic and worked at the American Museum of Natural History in New York. In 1907, Henson married Lucy Ross. After the last voyage, He published a book entitled *A Negro Explorer at the North Pole*. For such a pioneering explorer, Henson lived in relative obscurity, working in a garage and later at the U.S. Customs Bureau and the Post Office. Most of Henson's honors came late in his life. He became the first African American member of the elite Explorers Club in 1937. He received medals from the U.S. Congress, the U.S. Navy, and the Geographical Society of Chicago. In 1954, Matthew and Lucy Henson were received at the White House by President Dwight D. Eisenhower. Henson died on March 9, 1955, at age eighty-eight.

Billie Eleanora Holiday

Jazz Singer

1915–1959

Billie Holiday was born on April 7, 1915, in Philadelphia and given the name Eleanora Fagan. Her teenage parents, Sadie Fagan and Clarence Holiday, never married and her father, a banjo and guitar player in the famous Fletcher Henderson band of the early 1930s, barely acknowledged her during her formative years. Her mother brought her to Baltimore to live with relatives. Her grandfather was supportive, but other relatives were often insulting and abusive. While growing up in Baltimore she discovered she had an unusual voice and a love of music. Dreaming of show business, she changed her name to include the name of her screen idol, Billie Dove, and her father's last name. Her frequent rebellions led to time at the House of the Good Shepherd for Colored Girls. Nevertheless her singing career began in Baltimore when, in her early teens, she began performing in the waterfront entertainment district.

In 1929 she moved to New York to join her mother, and within a year she became a familiar voice in the Harlem night clubs. John Hammond, the jazz recording producer and critic first heard this exceptional teenager in 1933 singing at Monette Moore's club and wrote about her unusual voice and style in the British journal *Melody Maker*. Weeks later, Billie made her first recording singing two songs, "Your Mother's Son-in-Law" and "Riffin the Scotch." Her first movie performance came in Duke Ellington's 1935 short film *Symphony in Black* singing "Big City Blues." That year she also made the first of many performances at Harlem's Apollo Theatre.

One of her greatest musical feats was recording in 1939 the early protest song, "Strange Fruit," a challenge to lynching, with the Commodore label. Her contracting record company, Columbia records, refused to produce her recording of this song, but Holiday's message and dramatic rendition brought her greater admiration from fans around the world.

Singing with jazz bands led by Count Basie, Duke Ellington, Fletcher Henderson, Benny Goodman, Artie Shaw, and Ted Wilson brought her international fame. Toward the end of World War II, she recorded with Decca, which gave her the creative freedom she long desired. Her new musical style under this label included, "Lover Man," which quickly surpassed her other record sales. She appeared in the 1946–47 feature film *New Orleans*, but at the peak of her professional career, she became addicted to heroin and voluntarily entered a private clinic. Within weeks of her release she was arrested and sentenced for a year and a day in the federal penitentiary at Alderson, West Virginia. Ten days after her release, she performed before a packed audience at Carnegie Hall in New York City.

By the early 1950s, she remained without her Cabaret Performer's License and was viewed with disapproval by many of her former friends and fans. Nevertheless, she was still able to make highly successful European tours. French jazz enthusiasts referred to her as "the Princess of Harlem."

In 1958, she released her last album, "Lady in Satin," with orchestral arrangements by Ray Ellis. Her final appearance was early in 1959 at a benefit concert at the Phoenix Theatre in New York. Weeks later, on May 31, 1959, she became seriously ill and was taken to Metropolitan Hospital in Harlem where she was shunned as a drug addict and alcoholic. Almost penniless and alone, she died on July 17, 1959. She had reached the heights of her profession and captured the hearts of thousands around the world with her music. Billie Holiday was the standard by which jazz singers continue to be judged.

Lillie Carroll Jackson

Community Leader

1889–1975

Lillie Carroll Jackson led the struggle for equal rights as president of the Baltimore Chapter of the National Association for the Advancement of Colored People from 1935 until her retirement in 1970. She fought for educational and employment opportunities, open housing and recreational facilities, and federal civil rights legislation. Called "Fearless Lil," she worked with and prodded political leaders, especially Maryland Governor Theodore McKeldin.

Lillie Carroll was born on Greenwillow Street in West Baltimore on May 25, 1889, the seventh of eight children of Charles and Amanda Bowen Carroll. Her father, a former slave from Baltimore County was, according to family tradition, a descendant of Charles Carroll of Carrollton, a signer of the Declaration of Independence. Her mother, a teacher, grew up in Montgomery County. Lillie graduated from the Colored High and Training School in 1908 and taught second grade at the Biddle Street School. In 1910 she married Kieffer Jackson. They spent the next eight years traveling the country, speaking on religion and education. They had four children, Virginia, Juanita, Marion, and Bowen.

The Jacksons returned to Baltimore in 1918 to find the city's segregation practices harming their own children as well as all African Americans. Virginia and Juanita were denied admission to Maryland public universities and had to go to college in Pennsylvania. African Americans were routinely excluded from most major stores. Mrs. Jackson committed the rest of her life to a forceful and effective battle for full civil rights for African Americans. One of her favorite slogans was, "God helps those who help themselves," and she led the way in that effort. "Be somebody!" she told people, and she fought for the opportunity for everyone to do just that.

In 1935, Carl Murphy, of the *Afro-American* newspaper, asked Lillie to become president and direct a revival of Baltimore's moribund chapter of the NAACP. She agreed, and poet Langston Hughes wrote of the first woman president of a major NAACP chapter, "She lives, works, eats and sleeps the NAACP. It is her heart and soul." Jackson fought hard for appointments of black men and women as police officers, firefighters, librarians, and social workers. She then organized a school to prepare applicants for the required civil service exams. An important part of employment opportunity is education, and in 1935 the NAACP, with a team of lawyers headed by Charles H. Houston and including the young Thurgood Marshall, began a series of successful suits to force the University of Maryland to open its schools of Law, Medicine, Pharmacy, Dentistry, Nursing, and Engineering to African American students. Other efforts led to desegregation of schools, housing, and public facilities such as theaters, swimming pools, golf courses, tennis courts, and Maryland's state parks, which generally excluded blacks. In 1942 Jackson began a voter registration drive that resulted in major political victories during the 1950s. "Ballots, not bullets" were her key to power. During the heyday of the Civil Rights Movement, when volunteers were arrested during marches and sit-ins, she put up her own money for bail.

Lillie Carroll Jackson was the first woman trustee of the Sharp Street Methodist Church, where she was a lifelong member. In 1948 she was elected to the national board of directors of the NAACP. She was a member of the National Urban League, the National Council of Negro Women, and the YWCA. In 1956 she received an honorary Doctor of Laws degree from Morgan State College, and in 1957 she was selected the *Afro's* Mother of the Year. She is one of a small number of women in the Maryland Women's Hall of Fame. Lillie Carroll Jackson died in Baltimore on July 5, 1975. Her home at 1320 Eutaw Place became a Civil Rights museum.

Mary Elizabeth Lange

Religious Leader and Educator

1784–1882

Mary Elizabeth Lange founded and was the initial "Superior General" of the Oblate Sisters of Providence, the first predominantly African American Roman Catholic order to be established in the U.S. "Mother Mary" became one of the most highly respected African American religious and educational leaders in Baltimore. She led a small group of devoted Catholic women who founded the St. Frances Academy for Colored Girls on June 5, 1829, and with the support of the Archbishop of Baltimore, the sanction of the Holy See, and the Sulpician Order in Baltimore, began the Oblate Sisters of Providence. The school, located near Paca Street, began with twenty-four students, all French-speaking refugees from St. Domingue (now Haiti), who had fled their country's revolution. The Oblate Sisters of Providence survived the early years of personal hardship and expanded to serve the children of other cities, including Philadelphia, New Orleans, and St. Louis as well as those in nations in the Caribbean and Central America.

Mary Elizabeth Lange was born in 1784 in the French colony of St. Domingue to Clovis Lange, a plantation owner, and Annette Lange. According to one source her ancestry was part Jewish; according to another she was born a slave. In the aftermath of the St. Domingue slave uprising of August 1791 she fled with relatives to Cuba. In 1813 she left Cuba for Baltimore.

Young Mary Elizabeth attended St. Patrick's Roman Catholic Church in Fells Point, whose pastor, Monsieur Moranville, helped her adjust to life in America. After years of serious religious study (1813–1820) she conducted a small school for the children of the poorest French-speaking mothers. On June 12, 1828, Elizabeth helped establish a religious boarding school. Eager to further her work among the city's destitute, Father Joubert, a Sulpician Catechist, organized Elizabeth and two of her longtime associates, Marie Balas and Rosine Boegue, into a new religious order. After receiving Vatican approval, Elizabeth and four other novices took their vows, and the new order, the Oblate Sisters of Providence, was established on July 2, 1829.

The community's response to their school was so overwhelming that it soon had to move from Paca Street to a larger building on Richmond Street. The following year, 1830, an adjacent property was purchased. Church fathers appointed Mary Elizabeth the "Superior General" of the new order. Mother Mary Elizabeth also worked in the city's Almshouse for Colored People. By 1833, the work of the new order in caring for and educating women and children resulted in a large debt. Mother Mary Elizabeth donated $1,411.19 from her inheritance to pay it.

The order grew steadily. In 1855 it admitted ten additional sisters and increased its student enrollment to three hundred. Two years later, it opened two new schools for African American youth, the St. Joseph's School in South Baltimore and the St. Michael's School at Fells Point. Mother Mary Elizabeth served as Superior General of the order from 1829 to 1832 and 1835 to 1841. From 1851 to 1855, she also served as Novice Mistress. She helped open a home for widows in 1860 and during the Civil War worked as the local Superior of the St. Benedict's School.

The Oblate Sisters opened similar schools in New Orleans (1860) and Philadelphia (1865). Toward the end of the Civil War, the order created two new schools in Baltimore for orphaned black children, the Blessed Peter Clavier School and the St. Benedict's School. Mother Mary Elizabeth's work contributed to the phenomenal growth of Catholicism within Baltimore's African American community. As a consequence, in 1863 the St. Francis Xavier Catholic Church of Baltimore became the seat of the first parish for African American Catholics. She died in 1882 at the convent after serving in a variety of leadership roles for fifty-three years.

Reginald Francis Lewis

Businessman and Philanthropist

1942–1993

Reginald Francis Lewis was born on December 7, 1942, in East Baltimore, the only child of Clinton and Carolyn Cooper Lewis. At age five, his parents separated and his mother returned to her parents' home where he grew up with his maternal grandparents. He attended his neighborhood St. Francis Xavier Catholic School. When he was nine, his mother married Jean S. Fugett and before long Reginald enjoyed the arrival of five siblings. From an early age, he showed an interest in working hard with a clear business purpose. His first job was delivering the *Afro-American*, and later the *Baltimore News-American*, in his neighborhood. He referred to his earnings as "Reggie's Hidden Treasure." He excelled academically at Baltimore's Dunbar High School, then played quarterback for the football team, forward for the basketball team, and shortstop for the baseball team. He also waited tables in the evening and took on other jobs during the summer months, the most memorable at one of Baltimore's golf clubs.

In the fall of 1961, he entered Virginia State University on a football scholarship and majored in economics. In his second year, he decided to devote most of his time to his studies. Although it was a long shot for him to enter a top law school, Reginald was determined to do so and became one of a handful of minority students to enter Harvard University Law School in the fall of 1965. There Lewis prepared to attain his long-term goals. In the summer he returned to Baltimore to work in the law firm of Piper and Marbury. He focused on securities law and prepared his third-year paper on financial takeovers. He graduated with a law degree in 1968.

Lewis joined the prestigious New York City law firm of Paul, Weiss, Rifkind, Wharton, and Garrison. His fierce competitive nature led him to establish his own law firm, one of the first black law firms on Wall Street. At the same time, he involved himself in a number of civil rights issues. Among the most highly publicized was his role as the attorney for the U.S. Commission for Racial Justice and his work as the attorney for Benjamin F. Chavis. Chavis was implicated in the 1972 "Wilmington Ten" case involving civil rights activists and jailed for alleged conspiracy.

Lewis developed a specific strategy to be a major player in the takeovers of the 1980s. He first established the TLC Group Company in 1983 and acquired his first leveraged buyout of the New York–based McCall Pattern Company, one of the nation's oldest and second largest maker of home sewing patterns, for $22.5 million. The company had revenues of $51.9 million with profits of about $6 million. He sold it in June 1987 for $90 million, catapulting himself into the ranks of the country's financial elite.

His next effort focused on the Beatrice International Food Company, a food distribution company that also produced snacks and ice cream with holdings in thirty-one countries. Lewis completed the deal in October 1987 for $985 million and it became the largest buyout to that date of any American firm with large overseas assets. He had accomplished what few thought was possible for one from such humble beginnings. He also coauthored his inspirational autobiography entitled, *Why Should White Guys Have All the Fun? How Reginald Lewis Created a Billion Dollar Business Empire.*

On January 18, 1993, at the age of 51, Lewis died from brain cancer diagnosed only the year before, leaving his wife, Loida N. Lewis and his half-brother, Jean S. Fugett, Jr. to carry on the successes he initiated in corporate America. His net worth exceeded $400 million, and he had donated $1 million to Howard University, $100,000 to the University of the Phillipines, $3 million to Harvard University, and $2 million to the NAACP.

Thurgood Marshall

Supreme Court Justice

1908–1993

Thurgood Marshall was born in Baltimore on July 2, 1908. He attended public schools and graduated from Frederick Douglass High School and Lincoln University in Pennsylvania. In 1929 he married Vivian "Buster" Burey, and in 1933 graduated first in his class from Howard University Law School. The University of Maryland School of Law had denied him admission because he was black. After passing the Maryland bar exam, he opened a small office and helped clients whether they could pay or not.

Marshall represented the *Afro-American* newspapers and the local chapter of the NAACP. Legal victories included a suit to equalize the pay of black and white teachers in the Anne Arundel County public schools and a suit to open Baltimore's public golf courses to all players. In 1935 he helped win the important case of *Murray v. Maryland*, forcing the University of Maryland School of Law to admit a young black student, Donald Murray. Marshall shrewdly based his strategy on the 1896 Supreme Court case of *Plessy v. Ferguson*, which permitted separate but equal facilities. Clearly, no other school could provide equal training for a future Maryland lawyer, since the University of Maryland was the only law school in the state.

Thurgood accepted a job in the national office of the NAACP and in 1940 became director-counsel of the newly created NAACP Legal Defense and Education Fund. In twenty-one years, he argued thirty-two cases before the Supreme Court, winning twenty-seven. He went to Korea and Japan to investigate racism in the armed forces and risked his life traveling in sections of this country that did not welcome change. Marshall's best known case was *Brown v. Board of Education of Topeka* in which he won a 9–0 Supreme Court directive ending legal segregation in public schools throughout the nation. Chief Justice Earl Warren concluded in the 1954 decision that "separate facilities are inherently unequal." This precedent was later used to desegregate many other public facilities.

Marshall's wife died shortly after the *Brown* decision. He had stayed home and taken care of her during her illness. In December 1955 he married Cecilia "Cissy" Suyat, a fellow NAACP employee who had been born in Hawaii of Filipino ancestry. They had two children, Thurgood, Jr. and John.

In 1962, President John F. Kennedy appointed Marshall to the U.S. Second Circuit Court of Appeals in New York City. In 1965 President Lyndon B. Johnson made Marshall United States Solicitor-General, an office in which he would enforce the many new civil rights laws.

Johnson nominated Thurgood Marshall to become the first African American Supreme Court Justice, an appointment the Senate confirmed on August 30, 1967. In his statement, Marshall said, "Let me take this opportunity to reaffirm my deep faith in this nation and its people and to pledge that I shall be ever mindful of my obligation to the Constitution and to the goal of equal justice under law." Marshall served on the highest court of the land until his retirement in 1991. He regularly took positions in favor of desegregation, against capital punishment, and in favor of a woman's right to choose.

Thurgood Marshall remained a man of the people. He played poker with notables such as Ralph Bunche and Morgan State College President Martin Jenkins. He met his old high school friend Cab Calloway at the horse races. He enjoyed westerns and baseball. Thurgood Marshall's contributions as an advocate and as a judge make him forever a major figure in American jurisprudence. He died on January 24, 1993, in Bethesda, Maryland.

Clarence Maurice Mitchell, Jr.

Journalist, Lawyer, and Lobbyist

1911–1984

Clarence Mitchell, Jr., dedicated his life to "working for the right of all men to share in the blessing of our Constitution." Mitchell led a revolution. During his years as director of the Washington bureau of the National Association for the Advancement of Colored People, he was known as the "101st Senator" because of his knowledge and effectiveness. When he retired in 1978, the United States was a very different place because of his work.

He was born on March 8, 1911, the son of Elsie and Clarence Mitchell of Stockton Street in West Baltimore. The family's house on Bloom Street, their first with indoor plumbing, was in a racially integrated working-class neighborhood. Clarence attended Carey Street Elementary School and graduated from Douglass High School. His father worked as a waiter at the Rennert Hotel. His mother toiled as a laundress, a hot, heavy job that allowed her to work at home and keep a watchful eye on her children. Young Clarence delivered ice in the summer and coal in the winter, and worked in a bakery, a confectionery store, and as an elevator operator. The family used the Pitcher Street library and attended St. Katherine's Episcopal Church. Mitchell graduated from Lincoln University in 1932 and from the University of Maryland School of Law in 1962. In 1938 he married Juanita Jackson. They had four sons: Clarence M. III, Keiffer, Michael, and George.

After college, Mitchell was hired as a reporter for the Baltimore *Afro-American*. In 1937, the Urban League awarded Mitchell a fellowship to the Atlanta School of Social Work and the following year hired him as executive secretary of its new St. Paul, Minnesota, office. In 1941, Mitchell moved to Washington and joined Mary McLeod Bethune, Robert Weaver, and others in developing wartime fair employment programs. After World War II, he became labor secretary of the National Association for the Advancement of Colored People.

In 1950, Clarence Mitchell was selected as director of the NAACP Washington Bureau, and became the nation's leading civil rights lobbyist. He mastered the details of congressional rules, specifics of bills, and the inner workings of the political system. He formed alliances with sympathetic senators and congressmen, organized labor, white liberals, and Christian and Jewish groups.

Victories included a Civil Rights Act in 1957, the first since Reconstruction, and major legislation during Lyndon Johnson's presidency. The comprehensive Civil Rights Act of 1964 made the federal government responsible for protecting the rights of all citizens, including women and all racial, ethnic, and religious groups in employment, voting, the use of public facilities, education, and federal spending. After television showed violent attacks against blacks trying to register to vote, the Voting Rights Act of 1965 sent federal registrars into problem states. In 1968, the Fair Housing Act made discrimination in the sale and rental of most housing illegal. During President Jimmy Carter's administration, Mitchell's victories included a strengthened Equal Employment Opportunity Commission, Youth Unemployment Projects that hired 750,000 young people—including 300,000 African Americans—set-asides for minority companies in public works contracts to help the growth of minority-owned businesses, and appointments of increased numbers of women and minorities to high government positions.

In 1978, Mitchell retired from the NAACP, joined the family's Baltimore law firm, and wrote a column for the *Baltimore Sun*. He received the 1967 Spingarn Medal, the highest award given by the NAACP, the Presidential Medal of Freedom, and many honorary degrees. Clarence Mitchell died on March 18, 1984, at his home on Druid Hill Avenue. On March 8, 1985, the Clarence M. Mitchell, Jr., Courthouse was dedicated in downtown Baltimore.

Carl John Murphy

Publisher and Activist

1889–1967

Carl Murphy was an extraordinary journalist, educator, publisher, and community activist. His professional career began as a college professor at Howard University. He then joined his father's newspaper, the Baltimore *Afro-American,* and launched a journalistic career that focused attention on critical Civil Rights issues in Maryland. He became one of the most ardent supporters of the NAACP within Baltimore and throughout Maryland. He was in the forefront of the struggle to end segregation in Maryland and across the U.S. He was also one of the great promoters for the integration of Maryland higher education. At the same time, he became one of the primary architects for the expansion and economic restructuring of Maryland's premier historically black institution of higher education, Morgan State University.

Carl John Murphy was born in Baltimore on January 17, 1889, to John Henry (senior) and Martha Howard Murphy. On completion of high school in Baltimore, Carl studied at Howard University and graduated in 1911. He next enrolled in the graduate school at Harvard University, completing his master's degree in 1913. He would later continue his postgraduate work at the University of Jena in Germany. On earning his Harvard degree, Carl became professor of German and chairman of the Foreign Languages Department at Howard, and he taught there from 1913 to 1918. He then changed careers, relinquishing his college teaching and joining the staff of his father's newspaper.

For the next four years, Carl immersed himself in his new career, learning all aspects of the newspaper business so that when his father died in 1922 he assumed the position of publisher and editor of the paper, a position he would hold for the next thirty-nine years. During that time he made the newspaper into one of the largest circulating and most financially successful African American–owned and operated businesses in the nation. The paper was published twice weekly in Baltimore and Washington, D.C., and weekly in Philadelphia, Richmond, and Newark, carrying the news that directly affected the African American communities.

Carl Murphy was also extremely committed to improving race relations in Baltimore, the state, and the nation. He was a strong supporter of the NAACP, especially the work of Charles Houston and Thurgood Marshall, serving on the organization's board of directors and chairing a number of its committees. He gave of his time, talents, and financial resources, particularly in the area of public school desegregation, from the Donald Murray case in 1935 to the Supreme Court's 1954 *Brown v. Board of Education* decision. For his efforts, he received the 1954 America Teamwork Award of the National Urban League. He played a leading role in desegregating the city's restaurants, department stores, and theaters.

Murphy was also a driving force behind the consolidation and further development of Morgan College. In 1939 he was a key player in the effort to change the private status of the institution and make it into a state college. He became a charter member of the new board of trustees and in 1953 became the college's first African American chair of that board. So instrumental was he in developing the faculty and facilities during the 1950s that the college named its Fine Arts auditorium and complex after him. He envisioned Morgan becoming the leading African American institution of higher learning in the state of Maryland. He died on February 26, 1967, having made a lasting and significant contribution to the betterment of all Marylanders.

John Henry Murphy, Sr.

Journalist and Businessman

1840–1922

J ohn Murphy was the first of his family to own and publish the Baltimore *Afro-American* newspaper, one of the oldest, largest, and most influential black-owned newspapers in the nation. Read by generations of Baltimoreans and East Coast readers, the *Afro* has served the community by promoting racial equality, by educating its readers, and by printing news of the African American community that was not available elsewhere.

John Henry Murphy, Sr., was born a slave in Baltimore in 1840. His father was Benjamin Murphy, who worked as a whitewasher, and his mother was Susan Coby Murphy. During the Civil War, John Murphy served in the 30th Regiment of U.S. Colored Troops and fought under Generals Ulysses S. Grant and William T. Sherman. After the war, Murphy, now a free man, worked as a whitewasher and married Martha Howard. Later Murphy, an active Republican, worked for the U.S. Postal Service, ran a feed shop, and eventually became a printer. Active at Bethel African Methodist Episcopal Church, Murphy became a district Sunday school superintendent. In that capacity, he established a newspaper, the *Sunday School Helper*. Soon he was hired to supervise the printing presses and the commercial printing operation of the small *Afro-American* newspaper started by Rev. William Alexander of the Sharon Baptist Church. Murphy bought the presses for $200 and in 1897 became owner and publisher of the *Afro*. Three years later, another small newspaper, the *Ledger*, founded by the Rev. George Freeman Bragg, Jr., of the St. James Episcopal Church, merged with the *Afro*. Bragg was editor and Murphy was business manager. Bragg left the *Afro* in 1915 and in 1918 John's son, Carl, left his faculty position at Howard University to take over as editor. John Murphy and his family maintained financial control of the company although other prominent black Baltimoreans also owned stock.

Under John Murphy the *Afro* distinguished itself in the world of journalism. In that time of segregated education, the *Afro* campaigned for equal educational facilities for black children, for equity in teachers' salaries, and for black membership on the Baltimore school board. The paper fought successfully to maintain the right of Maryland black men to vote at a time when other states were passing disenfranchisement laws. He campaigned for a fair share of government jobs for African Americans who paid their taxes but received few positions. The *Afro* opposed segregation in real estate ownership and by railroad and steamship lines. It urged community support of black-owned businesses as well as institutions such as Morgan College and Provident Hospital and covered the activities of local churches and fraternal organizations, whose members provided a steady readership.

The *Afro* covered national and international news. Because of Theodore Roosevelt's support for African American advancement, John Murphy endorsed him for president of the United States. The paper reported on African American participation in World War I, including the training of black officers and the heroism of units fighting in France. It covered Booker T. Washington and W. E. B. Du Bois they debated the best route to progress. Murphy supported Washington, who favored economic growth, but also praised Du Bois and his work for political empowerment and development of an educated leadership. Murphy began coverage of events in countries such as Haiti and Liberia, where people of African descent held political power.

John Henry Murphy died in 1922. The family selected his son, Carl Murphy, to run the newspaper, because of his abilities as editor and businessman. John Murphy's descendents have continued to operate the *Afro* and to speak out for the African American community.

Pauli Murray

Lawyer, Professor, and Priest

1910–1985

A woman of strong determination and deep faith, Pauli Murray moved Eleanor Holmes Norton to write that she "lived on the edge of history, seeming to pull it along with her. She was a civil rights activist before there was activism, and a feminist when feminists could not be found."

Anna Pauline Murray was born in Baltimore on November 20, 1910, to William Murray, a teacher from Reisterstown, and Agnes Fitzgerald Murray, a nurse. Baptized at St. James Episcopal Church, she was only three when her mother died. She grew up with her Fitzgerald aunts and grandparents in Durham, North Carolina. There she learned the interracial heritage of her grandfather's family, Pennsylvania farmers who moved to North Carolina to open a school during Reconstruction. That she accepted, but not the rape of her slave great-grandmother by the owner's son, and she felt ambivalence toward the white aunt who had raised the mixed-race children. Pauli wrote a moving family history, *Proud Shoes*, long before such works were popular.

Pauli graduated from New York's Hunter College in 1933, worked for the Works Progress Administration, then applied to graduate school at the University of North Carolina, which her white ancestors had generously funded. She was rejected because of her race. In 1940 she challenged segregation on an interstate bus traveling through Virginia and spent Easter in jail. When Harvard Law School rejected her because of her sex, she graduated from Howard University Law School with honors and as president of the class of 1944. In Washington she participated in successful sit-ins at several restaurants. She asserted that "one person plus a typewriter constitutes a movement" and reached Eleanor Roosevelt with her letters. They became lifelong friends.

In 1951, Murray published *States' Laws on Race and Color*, a major reference that Thurgood Marshall gave to every member of the NAACP legal staff. In 1960 she left the New York law firm where she worked to become a senior lecturer at the University of Ghana Law School and coauthored *The Constitution and Government of Ghana*, the only such reference available in 1961.

In 1965, Pauli earned a doctorate in juridical science from Yale. A founder of the National Organization of Women, she wrote in an article in the December 1965 George Washington University *Law Review* that, "the rights of women and the rights of Negroes are only different phases of the fundamental and indivisible issue of human rights." She wrote a brief for the American Civil Liberties Union challenging an Alabama law that allowed only white men to serve on juries. The unanimous 1966 federal court decision, based on the Fourteenth Amendment, found that there should be neither racial nor sexual bias in jury selection. From 1968 to 1973, Dr. Murray was professor of American Studies at Brandeis University, where she developed popular courses on law, politics, and society.

After the death of a friend, Pauli entered General Theological Seminary in New York at age sixty-two. She completed her field education at St. Philip's Chapel in Aquasco, Prince George's County, Maryland, then was ordained in the Washington Cathedral on January 8, 1977, the first black woman Episcopal priest in America. She celebrated her first communion in Durham at the Chapel of the Cross, where her grandmother Fitzgerald had been baptized. "All the strands of my life had come together," she wrote that day. "Descendent of slave and slave owners . . . now I was empowered to minister the sacrament of One in whom there is no north or south, no black or white, no male or female — only the spirit of reconciliation drawing us all towards the goal of human wholeness." Pauli served in four churches, including the Church of the Holy Nativity in Baltimore, before she died in July 1985.

Isaac Myers

Labor Leader and Businessman

1835–1891

Isaac Myers was born in Baltimore on January 13, 1835, to poor free parents. Maryland laws did not permit him to attend the Baltimore schools, so his parents sent him to the private day school operated by the Reverend John Forte, a black Methodist Episcopal minister. At age sixteen he began an apprenticeship with James Jackson, who would become one of the city's leading African American ship caulkers during the 1850s. Myers became a skilled caulker and one of the leading African Americans in Baltimore.

During the 1860s, white dock workers sought to eliminate African Americans working in the caulking trade, sometimes resorting to violence to get their message across. A few months after the Civil War ended, white caulkers and ship carpenters went on strike, insisting that all African Americans working as caulkers and longshoremen should be discharged. Supported by the city government and police, they drove African Americans from their jobs in the shipyards. In response, Myers proposed that African American caulkers form a union to purchase a shipyard and railway that they could operate cooperatively. The response was overwhelming and the pioneering venture quickly raised $10,000 within the African American community. They borrowed another $30,000 and secured a six-year mortgage. They then purchased an extensive shipyard and railway on February 12, 1866, and within six months the Chesapeake Marine Railway and Dry Dock Company employed more than three hundred African American workers at an average salary of $3 per day, an excellent wage for the times. Soon afterward, Myers became the president of the Colored Caulkers Trade Union Society of Baltimore. Because of his demonstrated commitment and vision for expanding the role of African Americans in trade unions, he was elected president of the National Labor Union representing African American unions across the country, and served until this union's demise in 1871.

Myers became a leading member of Baltimore's Bethel A.M.E. Church and for fifteen years was superintendent of Bethel's Sunday school. He was married twice, first to Emma V. Myers (d. 1868), and second to Sarah Deaver Myers. He became a Grand Master of the Maryland Masons. He was also a member of the Odd Fellows and the Good Samaritans. He wrote a publication called the *Mason's Digest* and tried his hand at drama, completing a three-act play, *The Missionary*. Between 1872 and 1879, he was employed in Baltimore's Post Office. For a couple of years, he also operated a coal yard but discontinued this venture to become a United States gauger, inspecting bulk goods entering the port of Baltimore between 1882 and 1887. This job gave him great insight into helping members of the African American community start and run their own businesses. In 1882 he became editor of the *Colored Citizen*, a weekly paper in Baltimore. In 1888, Myers was elected secretary of the Republican Party in Maryland.

Myers always sought ways to organize African American business and economic ventures in the city of Baltimore. He successfully established and was president of the Maryland Colored State Industrial Fair Association, the Colored Business Men's Association of Baltimore, the Colored Building and Loan Association of Baltimore, and the Aged Ministers Home of the A.M.E. Church. He died on January 26, 1891, at his home at 1218 Jefferson Street in Baltimore. His funeral service, regarded as one of the largest for an African American of that time, was held at the Bethel A.M.E. Church on Saratoga Street. He was buried in the Laurel cemetery and was survived by his second wife, Sarah, and his son, George Myers.

James William Charles Pennington

Clergyman, Writer, and Abolitionist

1807–1870

James William Charles Pennington was born a slave in January 1807 to Nelly and Brazi Pennington on the plantation of James Tilghman in Queen Anne's County. He was originally named James Pembroke. At the age of two, he, an older brother, and his mother were given to his master's son, Frisby Tilghman, who lived in Rockland near Hagerstown. As he grew older, he was hired out and learned to be a stone mason as well as a blacksmith. Nevertheless, he fled Maryland and slavery around the time he turned twenty-one. As he traveled north, sympathetic Pennsylvania Quakers helped him. He quickly learned to read and write and became proficient in the study of languages, history, literature, and theology. He continued to study when he moved to western Long Island and to New Haven, Connecticut, where he studied at Yale University's School of Divinity. Although he was refused official admission to the seminary, and allowed to sit in on classes but not participate, he was permitted to withdraw books from Yale's library. In this manner, he continued his studies in Theology and developed into an effective preacher, first for the African Congregational Churches at Newton (1838–40) and later in Hartford (1840–47). He also served twice as president of the formerly all-white Hartford Central Association of Congregational Ministers. He was elected president of the Union Missionary Society, which promoted the ban on the purchase of slave-produced goods, and he performed the marriage of Frederick Douglass and his wife when they could not afford the marriage fee.

In 1841 Pennington published what is probably the earliest history of the African-American experience, *A Text Book of the Origin and History of Colored People*. Two years later, he made his first trip overseas, to Britain, representing Connecticut at the 1843 World Anti-Slavery Convention and serving as a delegate to the World Peace Society meeting in London. That July he preached at Queen's Street Chapel in London and later in Paris and Brussels.

In 1847 he became the pastor of the First Shiloh Presbyterian Church on Prince Street in New York, where he spoke out against the activities of the American Colonization Society. Two years later his autobiography, *The Fugitive Blacksmith, or Events in the History of James W. C. Pennington . . . Formally a Slave in the State of Maryland, United States*, was published in London and quickly followed by two more editions. Fearing capture after the Fugitive Slave Act became law in 1850, he left the country until payment of $150 was made to his former owner. During this second visit to Europe, and while still technically a slave, he received an honorary doctorate from the University of Heidelberg. On his return to the U.S., he openly opposed the colonization movement and defended thirty-five African Americans accused of subverting the "Fugitive Act" in the New York courts. He was officially manumitted on June 5, 1851, in Hartford, Connecticut.

In 1855, Pennington was one of those who organized the New York Legal Rights Association, which sued the Sixth Avenue Railroad Company for refusing to provide "public accommodations." The suit eventually opened up city transportation in New York. He grew increasingly militant, and in an essay in the *Anglo-African Magazine* on November 5, 1859 called for the country's religious leaders to help the slaves more directly. During the Civil War, he pastored Presbyterian churches in New York and New England, but he became ill and disillusioned. After the war, he retired to Jacksonville, Florida, where he died on October 22, 1870.

James Amos Porter

Artist and Art Historian

1905–1970

The work of pioneering art historian and artist James Porter spans six decades. He became the most significant African American art teacher of his generation, interpreting African American art and examining the African and Afro-Caribbean artistic traditions, and he helped to establish African American art history as a scholarly field. Porter participated in dozens of exhibitions over his long and very productive career that began with his works' appearance at the Harmon exhibition in 1929. He also authored many essays on African American art and artists. In 1943 he published the well-researched, *Modern Negro Art*, still considered a classic, authoritative work on this subject. Over his career, Porter received many awards, including Rockefeller Foundation grants in 1935 and 1945 and the National Gallery of Art Medal in 1966.

James Amos Porter was born on December 22, 1905, in Baltimore, the youngest of seven children of John Porter, a Methodist minister, and Lydia Peck Porter, a teacher. After attending preparatory schools in Baltimore, he entered the public schools of the District of Columbia in 1918, graduating with honors in 1923 from Armstrong High School. He entered Howard University with a scholarship and pursued a degree in Art. On graduating in 1927, he was asked to join the faculty to teach Art. While there he pursued further studies at the graduate level and received a masters' degree in Art History from New York University in 1937. He also studied in New York City at the Art Students League with Dimitri Romanowsky. Porter spent the summer of 1935 visiting museums in Europe and studied art at the Sorbonne in Paris as part of a Rockefeller Foundation Grant.

At the 1929 Harmon Traveling Exhibition, the first major exhibition of his work, he received "honorable mention" for three portraits. In 1933, *Woman Holding a Jug* won the Arthur A. Schomburg Portrait Prize. During the 1940 American Negro Exposition in Chicago, Illinois, Porter was invited to exhibit his paintings. His work was displayed in New York's Downtown Gallery, International House, and Reinhardt Galleries, and in Washington, D.C.'s National Gallery of Art, the Corcoran Gallery of Art, and the National Museum of American Art at the Smithsonian.

Professor Porter continued to teach at Howard University and became chairman of the Department of Art in 1953, a position he retained until his death in 1970. He studied and worked to preserve the art of the Caribbean. Toward the end of World War II he spent months in Cuba and Haiti studying and collecting valuable works that would enhance the university's collection of paintings from this part of the African diaspora. In 1963, Porter undertook a year-long study of art, architecture, artifacts, and culture in Portugal, Spain, Italy, West Africa, and Brazil. This was sponsored in part by a *Washington Evening Star* research grant. Porter was awarded the National Gallery of Art Medal in 1966 for his years of diligent and outstanding work.

Porter's paintings, which capture the life, action, and spirit of African American life, can be found in dozens of locations. Many are in private collections. Other works are at Howard University and Lincoln University, and at the Harmon Foundation, IBM, Hampton University, and the National Archives and Records Administration in Washington. The father of African American Art died on February 28, 1970, in Washington, where he spent most of his adult life. He was survived by his wife, Dorothy Louise Burnett Porter, the librarian, archivist, and curator of the Moorland-Springarn Collection at Howard University, and his daughter, Constance Burnett Porter Uzelac.

John Thomas Quander

Physician

1880–1910

The Quander family traces its beginnings in Maryland to Henry Quando and Margrett Pugg, slaves of Henry Adams of Port Tobacco, Charles County. According to Adams's will, filed on July 9, 1686, the couple was given their freedom along with household furniture and cattle. Soon after, Henry and Margrett Quando were legally married and had at least four children. They remained near where they had been slaves, farming leased land, growing tobacco, and raising livestock—a free African American family in what would later become Prince George's County. According to family tradition, Henry had been one of two slave brothers who arrived in Maryland from the Caribbean. One segment of the Quander family remained in slavery; a few were sold into Virginia, and some became the property of George Washington. The Quando brothers were among the few former Maryland slaves to retain a near rendition of their original African name, "Quando," which has been traced to the "Amkwandoh" family along the Cape Coast of Ghana, West Africa. The change to Quander began with the census of 1800.

John Thomas Quander was born in 1880 to Charles Henry Quander and Lucinda Hodge Quander, in the Rosaryville section of the African American town of Cheltenham in Prince George's County. Like generations of Quander fathers and sons, his father farmed tobacco while his mother cared for their fifteen children. After attending the segregated school in Cheltenham, John left his rural home to work at the Long Beach Hotel on New York's Long Island. In an 1899 letter to his sister, Emma Frances Quander, he described his new surroundings. "I don't like it up here at all," he began. "I [have] never seen such a dry, desolate, old place. I think this [is] a fine resort for invalids but the last place in the world for pleasure seekers. . . . I still hope to be able to go to Howard [University], though my savings are much smaller than I had hoped for."

John entered Howard University Preparatory School in Washington, D.C., and eventually graduated from the university's medical school in 1909, having achieved what no one in the Quander family had done before. Yet, his professional accomplishments had not come easily. Under the leadership of a new dean, Dr. Edward Arthur Balloch, a graduate of Princeton and a Fellow of the American College of Surgeons, Howard's School of Medicine improved greatly. It hired its first full-time, highly trained faculty, held most classes during the day, and constructed a new hospital facility to improve patient care and instruction for medical students and faculty.

Upon graduation, Dr. John Thomas Quander set up his medical practice in his native Prince George's County. He passed the examination given by the Maryland Board of Medical Examiners on June 22, 1909, and received his Maryland license to practice medicine on August 5, 1909. Dr. Quander opened his office next to the residence of his sister, Emma Frances Quander, at 1 John Street in North Brentwood, Maryland. He was the first African American doctor to serve this community in over thirty years and the second to be permitted to practice in the county. His sister and her husband, Jeremiah Hawkins, were rising Republican political figures in the county and owned a large dairy farm in Randallstown, later called North Brentwood.

After practicing his profession for a mere eight months, Dr. Quander died tragically of complications from tuberculosis on April 12, 1910. His funeral was held at St. Augustine's Roman Catholic Church in Washington, D. C. He was buried in the Mount Olivet Cemetery, in the presence of the large Quander family and many well-wishers, all of whom were shocked and saddened by his sudden departure in the prime of life.

Benjamin Arthur Quarles

Historian

1904–1996

Benjamin Quarles, who wrote that "Afro-Americans helped make America what it was and what it is," was one of the highly respected and most original historians of his generation. He showed that understanding African American history is essential to understanding the totality of American history. Quarles wrote in 1964, "Except for the Indian, the Negro is America's oldest ethnic minority. Except for the first settlers at Jamestown, the Negro's roots in the original thirteen colonies sink deeper than any other group from across the Atlantic." The work of this magnificent scholar, who shared his time and talent generously, influenced thousands of students.

Benjamin Arthur Quarles was born on January 23, 1904, in Boston to Arthur and Margaret O'Brien Quarles. He was the first-born in this working-class, biracial family. Trips to the public library marked the beginning of a lifetime of scholarship. After graduating from Boston's English High School, he worked as a waiter in Florida and as a crew member on ships that sailed the Atlantic Coast. No one had suggested that this bright young African American go to college. In 1927 he enrolled at Shaw University in North Carolina, from which he graduated four years later as valedictorian. He then went to the University of Wisconsin, where he earned a Ph.D. in history in 1940. His dissertation on abolitionist and statesman Frederick Douglass was published in 1948. *Frederick Douglass* was the first of Quarles's many books about African American history.

In 1935, Quarles returned to Shaw University to teach history. Two years later, he married Vera Bullock. Their daughter, Roberta, was born in 1938. The following year, he became professor of History at Dillard University in New Orleans. He served as secretary of the New Orleans Urban League and also as honorary consultant in American history at the Library of Congress. While Dr. Quarles was on sabbatical doing research and writing in Washington in 1950–51, his wife Vera died suddenly. The following year, he married Ruth Brett, who was Dean of Students at Fisk University. They met when she was proofreading the manuscript of his second book, *The Negro in the Civil War*. Their daughter, Pamela, was born in 1954.

Benjamin Quarles became a Marylander in 1953 when he was appointed professor and chairman of the Department of History at Morgan State College in Baltimore, where he was the first faculty member to be voted "Teacher of the Year." He was named Distinguished Professor by the State of Maryland. The renowned scholar continued to be a dedicated teacher, sharing his methods and research. He published twelve more books, including *The Negro in the American Revolution* (1961), *Lincoln and the Negro* (1962), *The Negro in the Making of America* (1964), *The Black Abolitionist* (1969), *Allies for Freedom: Blacks and John Brown* (1974), *The Black American: A Documentary History* (edited with Leslie H. Fishel, 1975), and *Black History's Antebellum Origins* (1979).

Quarles served as vice president of the Urban League, as vice president of the Association for the Study of Negro Life and History, and as chairman of the State of Maryland Commission on Negro History and Culture. He retired from full-time teaching in 1974. During his lifetime, he received honorary degrees from seventeen universities, including Bowie State, Howard, Lincoln, Maryland, Morgan, the University of Pennsylvania, Rutgers, Salisbury State, Shaw, and Wisconsin. In 1988, Quarles was given the American Historical Association's Senior Historian Scholarly Distinction Award and in 1996 the Smithsonian Institution's National Museum of American History Lifetime Achievement Award. His later retirement years were spent with his wife Ruth in Mitchellville, Prince George's County. He died on November 16, 1996.

Vivien T. Thomas

Surgical Technician, Researcher, and Instructor

1910–1985

Vivien Thomas was born in New Iberia, Louisiana, on August 29, 1910. His mother was a seamstress, his father a carpenter who ran a contracting business. When Vivien was a boy, the family moved to Nashville, Tennessee, where he attended public schools. The Thomas children worked for their father, were paid, and in turn paid for their own clothes and other purchases. Thomas also worked as an orderly in an infirmary. Greatly inspired by his family doctor, Vivien saved $350 and in 1929 enrolled at Tennessee Agricultural and Industrial College as a pre-med major. He had completed one semester when the stock market crashed, wiping out his savings.

As the Great Depression began, Thomas left college and found work with Dr. Alfred Blalock at Vanderbilt University Hospital—the beginning of a lifelong partnership between the two men. Blalock conducted experiments utilizing traumatic shock theory, which laid the groundwork for blood transfusions that saved the lives of soldiers during World War II and many others since. In 1933, Thomas married Clara Flanders from Macon, Georgia. They had two daughters, Olga and Theodosia. In 1940, Blalock was invited to the Johns Hopkins Hospital in Baltimore to chair the Department of Surgery. Blalock agreed to go to Hopkins only if Vivien Thomas also was hired.

Thomas came to Hopkins in 1941 as Surgical Technician in Research. There were no other African American professionals at Hopkins, and Baltimore's housing segregation made it difficult to find a decent home. Thomas worked with Alfred Blalock and Dr. Helen Taussig, and conducted research that would later bring him great acclaim. Pediatric cardiologist Helen Taussig had pioneered surgical techniques to aid children born with "blue baby" syndrome. These children have a congenital heart deformity that prevents the heart from pumping enough blood to the lungs. Children who survived infancy were too weak to exercise and did not survive to adulthood. Vivien Thomas developed surgical procedures to bypass the problem area and, in November 1944, Blalock performed the first "blue baby" operation. Thomas's technical advances helped set the course for modern cardiac surgery. He kept meticulous records so that his research would be fully documented and useful to all who read it. In 1944, Blalock was asked to perform emergency surgery on a 15-month-old girl who weighed only nine pounds. Blalock insisted that Thomas be with him in the operating room, and they conferred on every step of the successful surgery. Their partnership continued through the many operations that followed.

Vivien Thomas trained young doctors in the intricacies of heart surgery. His students included internationally famous Denton Cooley and Levi Watkins, the first African American surgical resident on the Hopkins staff. Thomas also made a point of training young African Americans as technicians and hired high school students to work in his lab. Finally, after almost three decades at Hopkins, Thomas began to receive recognition for his brilliant work. In 1969, a group of former surgical residents commissioned a portrait of Thomas that now hangs at the Hopkins hospital. In 1976, Thomas was awarded an honorary doctorate of laws from Hopkins and was appointed Instructor of Surgery. Thomas worked at Johns Hopkins from 1941 to 1979. When he retired, he was made Instructor Emeritus in Surgery, an honor reserved for highly respected faculty members. Vivien Thomas died in Baltimore on November 26, 1985. He has been acclaimed for his pioneering research, his development of improved surgical techniques, and his teaching of young surgeons.

Harriet (Araminta) Ross Tubman

Abolitionist

CA. 1821–1913

Araminta Ross was born a slave on the plantation of Edward Broadus in Bucktown, near Cambridge, Dorchester County, on Maryland's Eastern Shore. She was one of eleven children born to Benjamin Ross and Harriet Green. At age five she was hired out and forced to work under harsh conditions. Defiant like her mother, she frequently rebelled and received brutal whippings, which scarred her neck and shoulders. Once an overseer threw a piece of iron that struck Tubman on the forehead and nearly killed her. Afterward, she at times experienced seizures. Her master eventually married her to John Tubman, in an attempt to make her a slave mother.

Her owner died in 1849. Fearing that she would be sold into the Deep South as many Maryland slaves were, she fled with two brothers, hiding in caves and graveyards during the day and traveling at night by the North Star. In order to avoid the slave catchers' dogs, she waded for hours in the waters of the Choptank River. Though her brothers gave up and returned to slavery, she pressed on, crossing the Delaware River with the aid of two Quakers, Ezekiel Hunn and Thomas Garrett, and finally reaching the safety of Philadelphia.

Soon Harriet was planning to rescue others from slavery, beginning with her immediate family. She knew slavery well, and preferred to start escapes on Saturday night, so that the fugitives were well on their way before startled owners could advertise the escape on Monday morning. With gun in hand she sometimes told her weary travelers there would be no turning back—they would "Live North or die here." Among her most daring feats was the successful attempt in 1857 to free her parents, who were advanced in age. Abolitionists called her the "Moses of her people." She supported John Brown's 1859 raid on Harpers Ferry, Virginia, although it was impossible for her to participate.

In 1860 she heroically defied the Fugitive Slave Act at the corner of First and Second Streets in Troy, a city in upstate New York. Tubman refused to allow southern slave-catchers to apprehend Charles Nalle, an escaped slave who had fled north. In spite of being "repeatedly beaten over the head with policemen's clubs," she refused to yield. In the ensuing riot, which Tubman helped to start, Nalle escaped to live the rest of his days as a free man.

During the Civil War, Tubman worked tirelessly for the Union. She probably followed General Benjamin F. Butler as he secured Maryland for the Union. Later she organized the African Americans on the Sea Islands off South Carolina and worked as a nurse in the Port Royal Hospital. She freed around 150 South Carolina slaves, who then joined Union forces. She remained ever committed to the fight for racial equality and was acknowledged for her work. Great Britain's Queen Victoria sent her a medal. During her later years, she was recognized as an American legend. Samuel J. May, a leading abolitionist, wrote, "She deserved to place first on the list of American heroines." But the U.S. government largely ignored her contributions until she died. In 1867 she married her second husband, Union veteran Nelson Davis. Twenty years her junior, he died in 1888. Tubman spent her last years promoting the Harriet Tubman House for Indigent and Aged Negroes in Auburn, New York. She also became active in the temperance and early women's rights movements.

Harriet Tubman died on March 10, 1913, at her home in Auburn, New York, and at last was honored by her government. She was buried with full military honors for her service to the country she helped to transform.

Phyllis Ann Wallace

Economist

1921–1993

Phyllis Ann Wallace revolutionized American economic thought, especially during the 1970s and 1980s. Her insightful work regarding the economic treatment of women, teenagers, single parents, and especially African American working women helped change attitudes in American society. She addressed committee forums, university classrooms, board rooms, and occasionally courtrooms across the country, often out of the limelight and glare of the media. She received numerous honors and honorary degrees, including the National Economic Association's Westerfield Award, and became the first woman president of the Industrial Relations Research Association.

Phyllis Ann Wallace was born on June 9, 1921, the first of seven children born to John and Stevilla Wallace. She attended Baltimore's Phillis Wheatley Elementary School, Booker T. Washington Junior High School, and Frederick Douglass High School. Her sister, Lydia, recalls her great love for reading. In 1939 she graduated from Douglass at the head of her class. This distinction should have allowed her to attend either the Johns Hopkins University, her first choice, or the University of Maryland, but the state's segregation in higher education prevented her from doing so. Consequently, she entered New York University, majored in economics, and graduated in 1943 magna cum laude and a member of Phi Beta Kappa. She was proficient in German, Russian, Spanish, and French but majored in economics simply because she wanted to do something very different from other women, who traditionally were pushed into education. She obtained her doctorate in 1948 from Yale with a dissertation on international trade relationships.

Wallace taught at the City College of New York from 1948 to 1951 before moving to Atlanta University in Georgia, where she taught from 1953 to 1957. During the 1960s she left the classroom for the National Bureau of Economic Research. Her research focused on international trade and productivity issues. In July 1965 she was appointed chief of Technical Studies for the Equal Employment Opportunity Commission (EEOC). In this position, she accomplished her most compelling and pioneering work on the economics of job discrimination as it affected women and minorities in the American workplace. Between 1969 and 1972, Wallace served as vice president of research for New York City's Metropolitan Applied Research Center, where she traced the difficulties teenagers faced in the economy. Her extensive and carefully reasoned work helped create serious discussion and debate for the first time about this segment of the American economy. In 1972 she returned to the classroom as professor of economics at the Massachusetts Institute of Technology and stayed until her retirement in 1986.

Wallace was an activist-scholar whose efforts reached into corporate America as well as into many local communities. In the early 1970s she directed the research that led to the federal lawsuit charging AT&T, then the largest employer in the U.S., with sexual and racial discrimination. The 1973 landmark decision led to major socio-economic changes within corporate America, making wage scales for men and women equal for the same job. She served on numerous boards and advisory committees including the U.S. Department of Labor's Pay Advisory Committee and the Economic Advisory Panel of *Black Enterprise*. She was a member of the board of the Brookings Institution, Wellesley College's Center for Research on Women, and Boston's Museum of Fine Arts.

In the early 1990s, she helped to establish the Nubian Gallery in Boston and worked to raise funds to allow the children of Boston's poorer neighborhoods to view the collection. Among her most important publications are *Pathways to Work* (1974), and *Black Women in the Labor Force* (1980).

Augustus Walley

Buffalo Soldier and Army Officer

1856–1938

Augustus Walley was born to slave parents on March 10, 1856, in Reisterstown, Maryland. His mother was Annie Johnson, and he had one half-brother, John Wesley Johnson. By the end of the Civil War, Reisterstown had become the regular "stage stop" for most travelers going west from Baltimore City. There were inns, taverns, and establishments catering to the wagon, stage, and buggy business in the town along the mile-long main street. Persons of wealth frequented the Hitshoe Hotel and Forney's Tavern. Walley's interest in the U.S. Cavalry possibly began with his employment in the equestrian business of his home town. He seems to have had a strong desire to serve his country, for in 1878, soon after he became a legal adult, he enlisted in the U.S. Army and was selected for the 9th Cavalry, where he would serve for more than twenty years with great distinction.

Though efforts had been made as early as August 25, 1862, not until May 22, 1863, did the War Department fully authorize the enlistment of African American soldiers. By the end of the Civil War, nearly 200,000 men, many of whom were runaway slaves, had joined the Union army and navy to risk their lives for freedom.

After the war, African American troops were sometimes known as "Buffalo Soldiers," a term thought to have originated with the Plains Indians. Recruited from the 1870s, Buffalo Soldiers accounted for about 20 percent of the cavalry on the western plains. They served in segregated units and their main responsibilities were to accompany settlers traveling westward. They also protected cattle drives and railroad crews, built roads and telegraph lines, and were called upon to arrest cattle rustlers and bandits. African American cavalrymen formed the 9th and 10th Cavalry Regiments and participated in 177 campaigns against Indian tribes from Montana to Texas. They created an impressive but unpublicized record of valor. On October 1, 1890, Walley received the Medal of Honor for his bravery nine years earlier, in August 1881, during a fight against Apache Indians at Cuchillo Negro Hills, New Mexico.

Walley was with the Fifth Army Corps Cavalry Division when U.S. troops embarked to fight in Cuba under General Joseph Wheeler, a former Confederate general, during the Spanish-American War in the summer of 1898. Their ship left Tampa and anchored off Cuba on June 21, 1898. Walley later described how he became part of the Santiago campaign with instructions "to advance towards the interior of the country and drive the Spaniards from their position." His troop set out one evening along with Theodore Roosevelt's Rough Riders. The next morning they were "fired upon by the Spaniards." In the action that followed, Walley again distinguished himself by saving the life of one of Roosevelt's wounded troopers while under fire. "I remained on the firing line until 11 A.M. when the Spaniards retreated: I was in the engagement July 1st, 2d, and 3rd in the charge of the San Juan Hill." Walley remained in Cuba until U.S. troops were withdrawn on August 14, 1898.

Walley retired from the army as a first sergeant in 1907, but served his country again during World War I, then returned to Reisterstown. He seldom spoke even to his family about his heady years in the cavalry. He never married and lived quietly with his brother. He died on April 13, 1938, and his funeral service was conducted with great fanfare. Augustus Walley was one of three African American "Buffalo Soldiers" from Maryland to receive the Medal of Honor. The others were Sergeant Thomas Boyne of Prince George's County and Corporal William Wilson of Hagerstown.

Samuel Ringgold Ward

Abolitionist

1817–1866

Samuel Ringgold Ward was the second of three sons born to slave parents William and Anne Ward on October 17, 1817, on the Eastern Shore of Maryland. His older brother died prior to Samuel's birth, and Samuel's mother protected the sickly child with her life. When he was three his parents, fearful that they would be sold, fled with their children to Greenwich, New Jersey, where they lived among Quakers. When he was about nine, they again moved, to New York City, where young Ward enrolled in "the Mulberry Street School for Negroes" and associated with Henry Garnet and others from Maryland.

By 1833 he was teaching African American students and considering becoming a minister. In preparation, he briefly attended the Oneida Institute in Whitesboro, New York. Although he did not complete his formal studies, Ward developed into an exceptional public speaker and preacher. His abilities soon caught the attention of leading abolitionists Gerrit Smith and Lewis Tappan, and Ward was appointed traveling agent of the American Anti-Slavery Society in 1839. At the same time, he received a license to preach from the New York State Congregationalist (General) Association. He chose to be part of the more moderate branch of the New York Abolition Society and also became a founding member of the Liberty Party in 1840. Ward served as pastor of two all-white congregations in upstate New York between 1841 and 1846 and was also appointed one of the founding vice-presidents of the American Missionary Association.

During the presidential elections of 1848, Ward publicly refused to endorse Martin Van Buren for the Free Soil Party partly because of Van Buren's reluctance to abolish slavery in the District of Columbia. The following year, 1849, he publicly debated Frederick Douglass at the Broadway Tabernacle in New York. The men debated for hours before a large audience on the topic, "The Constitutionality of Slavery."

A year after passage of the 1850 Fugitive Slave Act, Ward helped to free a runaway slave from jail and get him to Canada. Word of his actions forced him to move to Canada himself. In 1853 he was one of the driving forces in establishing a college in Bermuda and became owner and publisher of the *Provincial Freemen* newspaper in Windsor, Ontario. Ward worked for the Canadian Antislavery Society but was dissatisfied. A prolonged throat infection led him to study medicine. When his voice returned, Ward made a two-year lecture tour of Europe and began to write his autobiography. A British Quaker, John Candle, offered him fifty acres of land in Jamaica, but Ward sailed for the island without finalizing the payment of a loan for £140 and was charged with swindling a London trader. With his reputation in decline on both sides of the Atlantic, he refused the entreaties even of Frederick Douglass to return to the U.S.

Ward settled in Jamaica with hopes of raising his family and living the simple life of a farmer, but his decision to lead a new congregation of Baptists in Kingston brought him financial hardship. Nevertheless, he became a powerful voice for the disfranchised of Jamaica. In October 1865, Jamaica was rocked by a bitter confrontation between poor black peasants and rich plantation owners. A bloody riot, followed by savage retribution on the part of colonial forces, resulted in the loss of hundreds of lives. Ward published his views on the incident in a work entitled *Reflection Upon the Jordan Rebellion* (1866). Ward died and was buried in Jamaica soon after its publication. Frederick Douglass called him "the greatest orator he knew," and added that "in depth of thought, fluency of speech, readiness of wit, logical exactness and general intelligence, Samuel R. Ward has left no successor among the colored men amongst us."

Daniel Bashiel Warner

President of the Republic of Liberia

1815–1880

Daniel Bashiel Warner was the third president of the Republic of Liberia in West Africa and one of that young country's most talented and versatile chief executives. Warner was born a free African American at Hookstown, Baltimore County, Maryland, on April 19, 1815. His father, Jacob Warner, had obtained his freedom the year before. In 1823, at the tender age of eight, Daniel emigrated with his family to the West African area that became Liberia, sponsored by the American Colonization Society, which encouraged free black Americans to resettle in Africa. They arrived in West Africa aboard the ship *Oswego*. Warner received his early education from his father as well as from the fledgling school in the settlement, then worked with his father in the lumber business before becoming a seaman. He rose to captain of the Liberian government schooner *Euphrates* patrolling the coastal waters in search of illegal slave trafficking, and in the late 1840s helped construct a shipyard to service ships traveling between Liberia and the rest of the world. Deeply religious, Warner believed that Christianity could help improve conditions throughout Africa.

Warner began his long and distinguished political career when the Republic of Liberia was officially founded in 1847. He represented Montserrado County in the country's first House of Representatives and became its first Speaker of the House. In 1855, Warner was the first mayor of the capital, Monrovia, and also served as the nation's second secretary of state, completing two terms before moving on to presidential politics. Warner served as vice-president for two terms, 1861–63 and 1877–80, and as president for two two-year terms, from 1864 to 1868.

During his two terms as president of Liberia, Warner dealt with a series of critical issues confronting the young African republic. Among the most important were attempts to end years of conflict and to integrate and educate the many indigenous ethnic groups that lived within Liberia's borders. Warner also standardized trading policies and created the important ports of entry law, restricting international commerce to six ports. He was also forced to negotiate a sensitive international dispute with the British. Warner felt that in order for the young republic to develop, it should continue to encourage immigration to Liberia. As vice president he had made bold efforts to recruit significant numbers of African Americans to settle in "our fatherland," but by the time he became president, American immigration to Liberia had all but ceased as a result of the Civil War. He promoted immigration to Liberia from the West Indies and in February 1864 issued "A Proclamation to the Brethren of the Antilles," encouraging their permanent settlement in Liberia. In a convincing effort to demonstrate his government's commitment, Warner had the Liberian government vote $4,000 for the project and offered twenty-five acres of land to each family that settled in Liberia. The most enthusiastic response came from the British West Indian colony of Barbados. On April 6, 1865, 346 persons left Barbados on the brig *Cora* for a new life in Liberia. Warner also promoted an aggressive foreign policy with many European powers. In 1866, a Russian ship paid an official inaugural visit to Monrovia, launching an ambitious program to link Liberian trade with more nations. Warner also introduced progressive educational policies, creating a secretary of education and a public school system with schools for girls and indigenous children.

After completing his term, Warner remained deeply involved in Liberian politics for the remainder of his life. He was reelected and served as vice-president in 1877. He died in office in 1880.

Ann Maria Weems

Abolitionist

1840–[UNKNOWN]

Ann Maria was the daughter of John and Arabella Weems, who with their children had been the slaves of the Charles M. Price family of Unity, and later Rockville, Maryland, in the heart of Montgomery County. Price was a notorious Maryland slave trader of the 1850s. Four of Ann Maria's brothers—Addison, Augustus, Tom, and Joseph—had been sold earlier into the deep South. Ann Maria had been forced to spend most of her hours from early morning to late evening in the house of her master as a domestic slave. Her parents had been manumitted and lived in nearby Washington, D.C., with another daughter, Catherine, and a baby brother, John Junior. In 1855, realizing that it was only a matter of time before this helpless slave girl would also be sold away from Maryland into the South like her brothers, a truly committed abolitionist, Jacob Bigelow, a lawyer and one of the founders of the Washington Gas Light Company, repeatedly tried to purchase Ann Maria from her master, but without success. Bigelow then had Ann Maria kidnapped and brought to his Washington house, where he hid her for weeks in the attic. Slave catchers and local police searched for her and paid visits to Bigelow's residence at Seventh and E Streets, N.W. The runaway notice detailing her escape and offering a reward of $500 for her capture and return to slavery ran in the *Montgomery Sentinel* and the *Baltimore Sun*. Price described her as "a bright Mulatto, [with] small freckles on her face, [a] slender person [with a] thick suit of hair, inclined to be sandy."

Secretly, Ann Maria had left Washington with her "conductor," "Dr. H.," a professor from one of Philadelphia's medical schools. With Ann Maria dressed as a coach boy and assuming the name "Joe Wright," the pair traveled by horse and carriage through Maryland, stopping at "underground" sites in Havre de Grace and Perryville before crossing the Mason-Dixon Line into Pennsylvania. Ann Maria stayed at the Philadelphia home of William Still, whose mother was a Maryland slave and who now worked for the Pennsylvania Society for the Abolition of Slavery. Seventeen years later, Still published an account of her feat in his 1872 book, *The Underground Railroad, A Record*. The book contained a portrait of her in disguise. Ann Maria and her conductor went on by horse and buggy to New York, where she stayed at the home of Reverend Charles Bennett Ray, a Congregationalist Minister and the corresponding secretary of the New York Vigilance Committee. From there she traveled to Canada by a train that stopped at Albany, Utica, Syracuse, Rochester, Buffalo, and Niagara Falls, where she was greeted by members of her family. Ann Maria's parents later joined her in Canada. Abolitionists and antislavery groups from as far away as Scotland and former Maryland slaves, including Reverend Henry Highland Garnet, raised funds to purchase the freedom of her siblings. Within three and a half years of Ann Maria's escape from Maryland, all her brothers had won their freedom. Her mother Arabella wrote to William Still, who had done so much to help free Ann Maria from Maryland, "I have just sent for my son Augustus, in Alabama. I have sent eleven hundred dollars which pays for his body and some thirty dollars to pay his fare to Washington."

By 1870, the Weems family left Canada and returned to Washington. Elisa Carbone, who wrote an excellent novel of Ann Maria's life for young readers entitled *Stealing Freedom* (1998), regrets in her "Author's Note" that she was unable to uncover more information about Ann Maria Weems. She remarks, "Sadly, by 1861, there is no longer any trace of Ann Maria herself." Nevertheless, Ann Maria's courage indicates that slaves everywhere, including Maryland, were eager to become free.

Verda Freeman Welcome

State Senator

1907–1990

The third of sixteen children, Verda Freeman was born on March 18, 1907, to James and Docia Freeman in Uree, later called Lake Lure, on a farm high in the Blue Ridge Mountains of North Carolina. Her mother died when Verda was a teenager, and Verda immediately assumed responsibility for raising her younger siblings. She attended public schools in North Carolina and Delaware. After seeing her father turned away from the polls by a white adolescent poll worker because of his race, she vowed, "When I grow up, I'm going to vote."

In 1929 she moved to Baltimore and enrolled at Coppin State Normal School, graduating with an associate's degree in education in 1932. In 1935, while teaching in the Baltimore City public school system, Verda married Dr. Henry C. Welcome, a British Honduran. She earned a bachelor's degree at Morgan State College in 1939 and a master's degree in education from New York University in 1943. She also did graduate work at Columbia and Howard Universities.

Welcome's political activism began in 1946 when was she a member of the Mayor's Advisory Committee for Urban Renewal in Baltimore. Later she became president of Baltimore's North West Improvement Association, which in the 1950s spearheaded the fight to lower racial barriers in Maryland's public places.

Her rise to political leadership was aided in the fall of 1958 by the Valiant Women's Democratic Club of Baltimore when she ran as a Democrat against powerful Jack Pollack and his hand-picked candidate in Baltimore's predominantly black Fourth Legislative District. She easily defeated Alvin "Mickey" Jones, built her own organization, and represented this district in the House of Delegates until she won the state Senate seat in 1962. Her election led to violence, and she survived an assassination attempt in April 1964, but she kept on working for the advancement of all Marylanders. "I don't give up easily," she told a *News-American* interviewer in 1972. "There is no such thing as I can't. . . . I am a living example."

Having been stung by discrimination while attending a Young Democrats convention on the Eastern Shore—she was denied restaurant privileges and given a room in the basement at an Ocean City motel—Welcome fought to open public accommodations to African Americans. She sponsored bills requiring equal pay for equal work for women, gun control legislation, and bills permitting residents to complete voter registration by mail. She was ahead of most anti-smoking activists in seeking to ban smoking in public places and worked to help Maryland comply with social reforms during the Civil Rights Era. She became a powerful and influential member of Maryland's Senate Finance Committee and during the mid-1970s worked to grant some of the state colleges, including Morgan State, formal university status. Among her numerous awards were honorary doctorates from the University of Maryland (1970), Howard University (1972), and Morgan State University (1976).

One of her most important actions as a Maryland senator came in 1967, when she sought to reverse the Miscegenation Bill that had been part of Maryland law since the days of slavery. Another political victory came in the 1966 gubernatorial election, when she crossed party lines and endorsed the Republican Spiro T. Agnew. Agnew defeated Democrat George Mahoney, a known segregationist and vocal opponent of open housing. Senator Welcome died on April 22, 1990, at the age of eighty-three, at the Liberty Medical Center in West Baltimore. Her funeral, held at the Grace Presbyterian Church on Banister Road, was attended by prominent Maryland politicians, who came to pay their last respects to a gallant and courageous colleague.

N. Louise Young

Physician

1910–1997

Dr. N. Louise Young led the way for African American women in the medical profession in Maryland. An obstetrician and gynecologist, she began her practice at a time when few women of any race were doctors and has been praised for encouraging and helping women to break into the field. Dr. Young's medical career lasted for fifty-two years.

Louise Young was born in Baltimore on June 7, 1910. Her father, Dr. Howard Young, operated a pharmacy on Druid Hill Avenue at Hoffman Street until his death in 1945. Her mother, Estelle Young, graduated from Spelman College and was a teacher before her marriage. In Baltimore, Mrs. Young was active in women's causes and established the Colored Women's Suffrage Club, which sought the vote for women. Louise's paternal grandfather, the Reverend Alfred Young, had been born a slave in Cambridge, Maryland. He graduated from Howard University School of Theology and served as pastor of the Sharp Street Methodist Church, one of the earliest African American congregations in Baltimore. Louise Young attended Frederick Douglass High School and Howard University, where she received a bachelor of science degree in 1927. She graduated from Howard University Medical School in 1930 and did her internship at Freedman's Hospital in Washington. She had hoped to return to Baltimore to intern, but at that time Provident Hospital, like many medical facilities, would not accept women staff members, and no other hospital in the city would accept blacks. From 1940 to 1945 she completed a residency in obstetrics and gynecology at Provident and eventually obtained staff privileges there.

In 1932, Dr. Young opened her medical practice on Druid Hill Avenue, above Young's Pharmacy. In later years, she had an office on Garrison Boulevard. In addition to her private practice, she served as physician to women students at Morgan State College from 1935 to 1940 and to girls at Douglass High School from 1936 to 1969. She was staff physician at the Maryland Training School for Girls from 1933 to 1940. During World War II she was chairperson for First Aid and Evacuation of Negro Women and Children in the case of a national emergency declared by the Maryland Council of Defense. She helped organize the McCulloh Planned Parenthood Clinic. Dr. Young was an associate staff member at North Charles General Hospital, a clinician and staff member at the Cancer Detection Clinic, a visiting obstetrician at Union Memorial Hospital, and a member of the courtesy staff at South Baltimore General Hospital. At Provident, Dr. Young served as assistant chief of obstetrics from 1945 to 1950 and chief of obstetrics from 1950 to 1952. She chaired the Provident Committee during 1948 and 1949 when the group raised over $9,000 from the Maryland Elks, enough money to open a blood bank.

Young served on the Mayor's Task Force on Civil Rights and on the Hospital Integration Subcommittee during Theodore McKeldin's administration. She was a member of the Maryland Committee for Passage of Abortion Laws, and chaired the Committee to Prevent Passage of Voluntary Sterilization Laws. She was a member of the American Medical Association, the National Medical Association, the Medical and Chirurgical Faculty of Maryland, the Medical Committee for Human Rights, the National Association for the Advancement of Colored People, the Elks, and the Alpha Kappa Alpha sorority.

Louise Young was married to Dr. Gilbert Caldwell. After his death, she married William E. Spencer, a public school administrator. Her hobbies included horseback riding and other outdoor activities. She was a longtime member of St. James Episcopal Church. Dr. Young died on September 22, 1997, after suffering from Alzheimer's disease.

Further Readings

Baker, George "Father Divine"

Burkett, Randall K., and Richard Newman, eds. *Black Apostles*. Boston: G. K. Hall, 1978.

Burnham, Kenneth E. *God Comes to Harlem*. Boston: Lambeth Press, 1979.

Johns, Robert L. "M. J. Father Divine, 1879–1965, Religious Leader." In *Notable Black American Men*, edited by Jessie Carney Smith. Detroit: Gale Research, Inc., 1999, 307–10.

Parker, Robert A. *The Incredible Messiah: The Deification of Father Divine*. Boston: Little, Brown and Company, 1937.

Weisbrot, Robert. *Father Divine and the Struggle for Racial Equality*. Urbana: University of Illinois Press, 1983.

Banneker, Benjamin

Allen, Will and Daniel Murray. *Banneker: The Afro-American Astronomer*. Salem, N.H.: Ayer Company, 1999.

Baker, Henry E. "Benjamin Banneker, The Negro Mathematician and Astronomer." *Journal of Negro History*, 2 (April 1918): 99–118.

Bedini, Silvio. *The Life of Benjamin Banneker: The First African American Man of Science*. Baltimore: Maryland Historical Society, 1999.

Johns, Robert L., and Ida Jones. "Benjamin Banneker." In *Notable Black American Men*, edited by Jessie Carney Smith. Detroit: Gale Research, Inc., 1999, 49–52.

Kyle, Robert. "Banneker Buyer Makes Long-Term Loan to Maryland Museum." *Maine Antique Digest* (February 1997).

Latrobe, John H. B. "Memoir of Benjamin Banneker." In *Maryland Colonization Journal*. Baltimore: J. D. Toy, 1845.

Lewis, David L. *District of Columbia*. New York: Norton & Co., 1976.

Litwin, Laura. *Benjamin Banneker: Astronomer and Mathematician*. Berkeley Hill, N.J.: Enslow Publishers, 1999. (Juvenile)

Pinkney, Andrea and Brian Pinkney. *Dear Benjamin Banneker*. New York: Harcourt, 1998. (Juvenile)

Bishop, William Henry

Brown, Philip L. *The Other Annapolis, 1900–1950*. Annapolis: Annapolis Publishing Co., 1994.

Cobb, William Montague. *Progress and Portents of the Negro in Medicine*. New York: National Association for the Advancement of Colored People, 1948.

McWilliams, Jane Wilson. *The First Ninety Years: Anne Arundel Medical Center, 1902–1992*. Annapolis: Anne Arundel Medical Center, 1992.

Blake, James Hubert "Eubie"

Berlin, E. A. *Ragtime: A Musical and Cultural History*. Berkeley: University of California Press, 1984.

Carter, Lawrence T. *Eubie Blake: Keys of Memory*. Detroit: Balamp Publications, 1979.

Elliot, William G. "Eubie Blake." In *American National Biography*, edited by John A. Garraty and Merrick C. Carnes. Vol. 2. New York: Oxford University Press, 1999, 918–19.

Kimble, Robert, and William Bolcom. *Reminiscing with Sissle and Blake*. New York: Viking Press, 1973.

Rose, Al. *Eubie Blake*. New York: Schirmer Books, 1979.

Bragg, George E.

Brackett, Jeffrey R. *Notes on the Progress of the Colored People of Maryland Since the War*. Baltimore: Johns Hopkins University Press, 1890.

Bragg, George E. *Men of Maryland*. Baltimore: Church Advocate Press, 1925.

Gatewood, Willard B. *Aristocrats of Color: The Black Elite 1880–1920*. Bloomington: Indiana University Press, 1990.

Hayden, J. Carleton. "George Freeman Bragg, Jr." In *Dictionary of American Negro Biography*, edited by Rayford Logan and Michael Winston. New York: Norton & Co., 1982.

McGlotten, Mildred L. "Reverend George Freeman Bragg: A Negro Pioneer in Social Welfare." Master's thesis, Howard University, 1948.

Bruce, John Edward

Bruce, John Edward. *A Tribute for the Negro Soldier.* New York: Bruce & Franklin, 1918.

Burkett, Randall K. *Black Redemption: Churchmen Speak for the Garvey Movement.* Philadelphia: Temple University Press, 1978.

Crowder, Ralph L. "John Edward Bruce, Pioneer Black Nationalist."*Afro-Americans in New York Life and History,* 11 (1978): 47–66.

Gatewood, Willard. *Aristocrats of Color: The Black Elite 1880–1920.* Bloomington: Indiana University Press, 1990.

Gilbert, Peter, ed. *The Selected Writings of John Edward Bruce, Militant Black Journalist.* New York: Arno Press, 1971.

Taylor, Durahn. "John Edward Bruce." In *Encyclopedia of African American Culture and History,* edited by Jack Salzman, David Lionel Smith, and Cornel West. Vol. 1. New York: MacMillan Library Reference, 1996.

Calloway, Cabell "Cab"

"Cab Calloway." In *Encyclopedia of African-American Culture and History,* edited by Salzman, Smith, and West. Vol. 7. New York: MacMillan Reference Library, 1996.

Calloway, Cab, and Bryant Rollins. *Of Minni the Moocher and Me.* New York: Thomas Crowell Co., 1976.

Carney-Smith, Jessie. "Cab Calloway." In *Notable Black American Men,* edited by Jessie Carney Smith. Detroit: Gale Research Inc., 1999.

Frentner, Shaun. "Cab Calloway. " In *Contemporary Black Biography,* edited by L. Mpho Mabunda and Shirelle Phelps. Vol. XIV. Detroit: Gale Research Inc., 1999.

Kernfield, Barry, ed. *The New Grove Dictionary of Jazz.* New York: MacMillan, 1988.

Southern, Eileen, ed. *Biographical Dictionary of Afro American and African Musicians.* Westport, Conn.: Greenwood Press, 1982, 71–62.

Cassell, Albert Irvin

Cassell, Charles I. "Experience Record of Albert I. Cassell, Registered Architect." Manuscript Division of Moorland-Spingarn Research Center, Howard University.

Fields, Louis C. "Albert I. Cassell." *Baltimore African-American Resource and Tourist Guide.* Baltimore: Louis Fields, 1996, 51.

Logan, Rayford, and Michael Winston. "Albert Irvin Cassell." In *Dictionary of American Negro Biography,* edited by Rayford Logan and Michael Winston. New York: Norton & Co., 1982, 97–98.

Coker, Daniel E.

Coker, Daniel. *Journal of Daniel Coker.* Baltimore: Edward J. Coale & John D. Toy, 1820.

Fulop, Timothy E. "Daniel Coker 1780–1846, Minister and Abolitionist." In *Encyclopedia of African American Culture and History,* edited by Salzman, Smith, and West. Vol. 2. New York: MacMillan Reference Library, 1996, 603.

George, Carol V. R. *Segregated Sabbaths.* New York: Oxford University Press, 1973.

Payne, Alexander. *History of the African Methodist Episcopal Church.* Nashville: Publishing House of A.M.E. Sunday School University, 1891.

Thomas, Betty. "Daniel Coker." In *Dictionary of American Negro Biography,* edited by Logan and Winston. New York: Norton & Co., 1982, 119–20.

Cole, Harry Augustus

Cummings, Elijah E. "Judge Harry Cole — A Man Who Kept the Faith." *Afro-American,* February 20, 1999, A5.

Hilson, Robert, Jr. "Judge Cole Recalled with Warm Memories." *Baltimore Sun,* February 20, 1999, 4B.

Milleman, Michael. "Cole Found Common Ground." *Baltimore Sun,* February 21, 1999, 1C.

Phelps, Shirelle, ed. "Harry A. Cole." *Who's Who Among African Americans.* New York: Gale Research Inc., 1997.

Siegel, Eric. "Judge Cole dies at 78," *Baltimore Sun,* February 15, 1999: 1A & 6A.

Craft, Silas Edwin

Craft, Silas. *The History of Blacks in Howard County, Maryland.* Columbia, Md.: Howard County Branch, National Association for the Advancement of Colored People, 1986.

"Craft, Silas." *Who's Who Among Black Americans.* Farmington Hills, Mich.: The Gale Group, 1994.

"Silas Craft: Pioneer in Education, Integration dies at 76." *The Washington Post,* January 14, 1995.

Cummings, Harry Sythe

Bragg, George F. *Men of Maryland.* Baltimore: Church Advocate Press, 1925.

Callcott, Margaret Law. *The Negro in Maryland Politics, 1870–1912.* Baltimore: Johns Hopkins University Press, 1969.

Chapelle, Suzanne E. G. *Baltimore: An Illustrated History.* Sun Valley, Calif.: American Historical Press, 2000.

Papers of Harry S. Cummings. MS 2961. Special Collections, Maryland Historical Society, Baltimore.

Greene, Suzanne E. "Black Republicans on the Baltimore City Council, 1890–1931." *Maryland Historical Magazine,* 74 (1979): 203–22.

Cummings, Ida Rebecca

"Citizens Laud 'Miss Ida' at Wednesday Funeral Sevices." *Baltimore Afro-American,* November 15, 1958, p. 1.

Papers of Harry S. Cummings. MS 2961. Special Collections, Maryland Historical Society, Baltimore.

Hollie, Donna Tyler. "Ida Rebecca Cummings." In *Black Women in America: An Historical Encyclopedia,* edited by Darlene Clark Hine. Brooklyn, N.Y.: Carlson Publishing, 1993.

" 'Miss Ida' Dies: Was First City Kindergarten Teacher." *Baltimore Afro-American,* November 10, 1958, 1.

Report of Colored Empty Stocking and Fresh Air Circle. n.d., Beulah Davis Room, Soper Library, Morgan State University, Baltimore.

Day, Leon

Ashe, Arthur. *Hard Road to Glory.Baseball: The African American Athlete in Baseball.* New York: Amistad, 1993.

Holway, John. *Blackball Stars: Negro League Pioneers.* Westport, Conn.: Meckler Corporation, 1988.

———. *Black Diamonds, Life in the Negro Leagues.* Westport, Conn.: Meckler Corporation, 1989.

Leffer, Robert. "History of Black Baseball in Baltimore from 1913–1951." Master's thesis, Morgan State University, 1974.

Moffi, Larry. *Crossing the Line: Black Major Leagues, 1947–56.* Jefferson, N.C.: McFarland, 1994.

Peterson, Robert. *Only the Ball Was White.* New York: McGraw Hill, 1984.

Riley, James A. *The Biographical Encyclopedia of the Negro Baseball Leagues.* New York: Carroll & Graf Publishers, 1994.

Douglass, Frederick

Blassingame, John W., ed. *The Frederick Douglass Papers: Speeches, Debates and Interview.* Vols. 1–5. New Haven: Yale University Press, 1979–92.

Blight, David W. *Frederick Douglass' Civil War: Keeping Faith in Jubilee.* Baton Rouge: Louisiana State University Press, 1989.

Davis, Ossie. *Escape to Freedom: A Play About Young Frederick Douglass.* New York: Puffin Books, 1990. (Juvenile)

Douglass, Frederick. *Life and Times of Frederick Douglass.* Hartford, Conn.: Park Publishing Co, 1881; Secaucus, N.J.: Citadel Press, 1983.

———. *My Bondage and My Freedom.* Urbana: University of Illinois Press, 1987.

———. *Narrative of the Life of Frederick Douglass.* Boston: St. Martin's Press, 1993.

Foner, Philip S. *Frederick Douglass: A Biography.* New York: Citadel Press, 1964.

Foner, Philip S. *Frederick Douglass on Women's Rights.* Westport, Conn.: Greenwood Press, 1976.

Graham, Shirley. *There Was Once a Slave . . . The Heroic Story of Frederick Douglass.* New York: Messner Inc., 1947. (Juvenile)

Huggins, Nathan. *Slave and Citizen: The Life of Frederick Douglass.* Boston: Little, Brown, 1980.

Martin, Waldo E., Jr. *The Mind of Frederick Douglass.* Chapel Hill: University of North Carolina Press, 1984.

McFeely, William S. *Frederick Douglass.* New York: Norton & Co., 1991.

Patterson, Lillie. *Frederick Douglass, Freedom Fighter.* New York: Dell, 1970. (Juvenile)

Preston, Dickson J. *Young Frederick Douglass: The Maryland Years.* Baltimore: Johns Hopkins University Press, 1980.

Quarles, Benjamin. *Frederick Douglass.* New York: Atheneum, 1948, 1968.

Fleetwood, Christian Abraham

Dunbar-Nelson, Alice, ed. *Masterpieces of Negro Eloquence.* New York: G. K. Hall, 1997.

Fleetwood, Christian. Papers of Christian Abraham Fleetwood Washington, D.C.: Library of Congress Manuscript Division.

Johnson, Charles, Jr. "Christian Abraham Fleetwood." In *Dictionary of American Negro Biography,* edited by Logan and Winston. New York: Norton & Co., 1982, 223–24.

Longacre, Edward G. *A Regiment of Slaves: The 4th United States Colored Infantry, 1863–1866.* Mechanicsburg, Pa.: Stackpole Books, 2003.

Wesley, Charles H., and Patricia Romero. *Negro Americans in the Civil War: From Slavery to Citizenship.* New York: International Library of Negro Life & History. Association for the Study of Negro Life & History, Publishers Co., Inc., 1967.

Frazier, E. Franklin

Edwards, G. Franklin. "E. Franklin Frazier." In *Black Sociologists, Historical Contemporary Perspectives*, edited by James E. Blackwell and Morris Janowitz. Chicago: University of Chicago Press, 1974, 85–117.

———. "E. Franklin Frazier." In *Dictionary of American Negro Biography*, edited by Logan and Winston. New York: Norton & Co., 1982, 241–44.

Frazier, E. Franklin. *Black Bourgeoisie*. Glencoe, Ill.: Free Press, 1957.

———. *The Negro Family in the United States*. Chicago: University of Chicago Press, 1939.

———. *On Race Relations: Selected Writings*. Chicago: University of Chicago Press, 1968.

Platt, Anthony M. *E. Franklin Frazier Reconsidered*. New Brunswick, N.J.: Rutgers University Press, 1991.

Gans, Joseph "Baby Joe"

Ashe, Arthur. *A Hard Road to Glory: A History of the African-American Athlete*. New York: Amistad/Penguin, 1993.

Bragg, George F. *Men of Maryland*. Baltimore: Church Advocate Press, 1925.

Early, Gerald. "Boxing." In *Encyclopedia of African-American Culture and History*, edited by Salzman, Smith, and West. New York: MacMillan Library Reference, 1996.

Henderson, Edwin, B. *The Negro in Sports*. Washington, D.C.: The Associated Publishers, Inc., 1939.

Jones, Carleton. "Back Tracks: Joe Gans, Baltimore Boxer." *Baltimore Sun Magazine*, September 18, 1988, 24.

Sammons, Jeffrey. *Beyond the Ring, The Role of Boxing in American Society*. Urbana: University of Illinois Press, 1988.

Garnet, Henry Highland

Ofari, Earl. *Let Your Motto Be Resistance: The Life and Thought of Henry Highland Garnet*. Boston: Beacon Press, 1972.

Litwack, Leon F., and August Meier, eds. *Black Leaders in the Nineteenth Century*. Urbana: University of Illinois Press, 1991.

Pease, Jane H., and William H. Pease. *They Who Would Be Free: Blacks' Search for Freedom, 1830–1861*. Urbana: University of Illinois Press, 1990.

Schor, Joel. *Henry Highland Garnet: A Voice of Radicalism in the Nineteenth Century*. Westport, Conn.: Greenwood Press, 1977.

Smith, James McCune. "The Sketch of the Life and Labors of Rev. Henry Highland Garnet: A Memorial Discourse delivered in the Hall of the House of Representatives, February 12, 1865." Philadelphia: J. M. Wilson, 1865.

Stuckey, Sterling. *Slave Culture, Nationalist Theory and the Foundation of Black America*. New York: Oxford University Press, 1987.

Swift, David E. *Black Prophets of Justice: Activist Clergy Before the Civil War*. Baton Rouge: Louisiana State University Press, 1989.

Harper, Frances Ellen Watkins

Christian, Barbara. *Black Women Novelists: The Development of a Tradition, 1892–1980*. Westport, Conn.: Greenwood Press, 1980, 1985.

Foster, Frances Smith, ed. *A Brighter Coming Day: A Frances Ellen Watkins Harper Reader*. New York: The Feminist Press at the City University of New York, 1990.

Harper, Frances Ellen Watkins. *The Complete Poems of Frances E. W. Harper*, edited by Maryemma Graham. New York: Oxford University Press, 1988.

———. *Lola Leroy or Shadows Uplifted*. New York: Oxford University Press, 1892, 1988.

Montgomery, J. W. *A Comparative Analysis of the Rhetoric of Two Negro Women Orators, Sojourner Truth and F. E. W. Harper*. Fort Hays: Kansas State College, 1968.

Rubiner, Joanna. "Frances Ellen Watkins Harper." In *Contemporary Black Biography*, edited by L. Mpho Mabunda and Shirelle Phelps. Vol. 2. Detroit: Gale Research Inc., 1997, 116–20.

Sherman, Joan R. *Invisible Poets: Afro-Americans of the Nineteenth Century*. Urbana: University of Illinois Press, 1989.

Shockley, Ann Allen. *Afro-American Women Writers, 1746–1933*. Boston: G. K. Hall, 1988.

Smith, Jessie Carney. *Notable Black American Women*. Detroit: Gale Research, Inc., 1992, 457–61.

Henson, Josiah

Beattie, Jessie Louise. *Black Moses: The Real Uncle Tom*. Toronto: Ryderson Press, 1957.

Cavannah, Frances. *The Truth About the Man Behind the Book that Sparked the War*. Philadelphia: Westminster Press, 1975.

Gysin, Brian. *To Master — A Long Good Night: The Story of Uncle Tom, A Historical Narrative*. New York: Creative Age Press, Inc., 1946.

Hartgrove, W. B. "The Story of Josiah Henson." *Journal of Negro History* (1918): 1–21.

Henson, Josiah. *The Life of Josiah Henson, Formerly a Slave and an Inhabitant of Canada, as Narrated by Himself.* Bedford, Mass.: Applewood Books, 2002.

———. *Truth Stranger Than Fiction: Uncle Tom's Story of His Life from 1789–1877/ Rev. Josiah Henson.* Nashville, Tenn.: Winston-Derek Publishers, 1997.

Henson, Matthew Alexander

Berton, Pierce. *The Arctic Grail: The Quest for the Northwest Passage and the North Pole, 1818–1909.* New York: Viking, 1988.

Counter, S. Allen. *North Pole Legacy: Black, White and Eskimo.* Amherst: University of Massachusetts Press, 1991.

Ferris, Jeri. *The Story of Matthew Henson: Arctic Explorer.* Minneapolis: Carolhoda Books, Inc., 1989. (Juvenile)

Gilman, Michael. *Matthew Henson: Explorer.* New York: Chelsea House Publishers, 1988. (Juvenile)

Henson, Matthew. *A Negro Explorer at the North Pole.* New York: Frederick Stokes, 1912.

Herbert, Wally. *The Noose of Laurels: Robert E. Peary and the Race to the North Pole.* New York: Atheneum, 1989.

Hudson, Wade. *Five Great Explorers.* New York: Scholastic, 1995. (Juvenile)

Pearson, Patricia A. "Matthew A. Henson." In *Notable Black American Men,* edited by Jessie Carney Smith. Detroit: Gale Research, Inc., 1999, 541–44.

Roylance, Frank. "Hero's Ship Comes In, After Years of Neglect." *Baltimore Sun,* November 17, 1998, 1B.

Holiday, Billie Eleanora

Chilton, John. *Billie's Blues, Billie Holiday's Story 1933–1959.* New York: Stein & Day, 1975.

Clarke, Donald. *Wishing on the Moon: The Life and Times of Billie Holiday.* New York: Viking, 1994.

Gourse, Leslie. *The Billie Holiday Companion, Seven Decades of Commentary.* New York: Schirmer Books, 1997.

Holiday, Billie, with William Dufty. *Lady Sings the Blues.* New York: Penguin, 1984.

O'Meally, Robert. *Lady Day: The Many Faces of Billie Holiday.* New York: Arcade, 1991.

White, John. *Billie Holiday: Her Life and Times.* New York: Neal, 1987.

Jackson, Lillie Carroll

"Dr. Lillie M. Jackson: Lifelong Freedom Fighter." *Crisis,* 82 (1975): 279–300.

Hathaway, Phyllis. "Lillie Carroll Jackson." In *Notable Maryland Women,* edited by Winifred G. Helmes. Cambridge, Md.: Tidewater Publishers, 1977, 187–91.

"Lillie Carroll Jackson, Mother of a Movement." *Baltimore Sun,* August 21, 1999, 12A.

Miller, Allison X. "Lillie Mae Carroll Jackson." In *Encyclopedia of African American Culture and History,* edited by Salzman, Smith, and West. New York: MacMillan, 1996, 1410.

Lange, Mary Elizabeth

Breslaw, Elaine and Joan A. Anderson. "Elizabeth Clovis Lange." In *Notable Maryland Women,* edited by Winifred G. Helmes. Cambridge, Md.: Tidewater Publishers, 1977, 208–13.

Morrow, Diane Batts. *Persons of Colour and Religious at the Same Time: The Oblate Sisters of Providence, 1828–1860.* Chapel Hill: University of North Carolina Press, 2002.

Phillips, Glenn O. "Maryland and the Caribbean 1634–1984: Some Highlights." *Maryland Historical Magazine,* 83 (1988): 199–214.

———. "Elizabeth Lange," *Black Women in the United States: A Historical Encyclopedia.* New York: Carlson Publishing, 1992, 695.

Sherwood, Grace. *The Oblates' Hundred and One Years.* New York: MacMillan, 1931.

Stiehm, Jamie. "Nun's Tribute is 171 Years in the Making." *Baltimore Sun,* February 14, 2000, 1B, 18B.

Lewis, Reginald Francis

Englelbourg, Saul. "Reginald Francis Lewis." In *American National Biography,* edited by James A. Garraty and March C. Carnes. Vol. 13 (1999), 597–98.

Lewis, Reginald and Blair S. Walker. *Why Should White Guys Have All the Fun? How Reginald Lewis Created a Billion Dollar Empire.* New York: John Wiley, 1995.

Martin, Larry L., ed. *African Americans in Business: The Path Toward Empowerment.* Washington, D.C.: Associated Publishers, 1998.

McDean, Henry C. "Beatrice: The Historical Profile of an American-Styled Conglomerate." In *American Business History: Case Studies,* edited by Henry C. Delkloff and C. Joseph Pusateri. New York: Garland Press, 1987.

Marshall, Thurgood

Adler, David A. *A Picture Book of Thurgood Marshall.* New York: Holiday House, 1997. (Juvenile)

Aldred, Lisa. *Thurgood Marshall*. New York: Chelsea House, 1990.

Davis, Michael and Hunter Clark. *Thurgood Marshall: Warrior at the Bar, Rebel on the Bench*. New York: Carol Publishers Group, 1994.

Fenderson, Lewis H. *Thurgood Marshall, Fighter for Justice*. New York: McGraw-Hill, 1969.

Haskins, James. *Thurgood Marshall: A Life for Justice*. New York: Henry Holt & Co., 1992.

Kent, Deborah. *Thurgood Marshall and the Supreme Court*. New York: Grolier Children's Press, 1997. (Juvenile)

Marshall, Thurgood. *Racial Equality, Criminal Proceedings and the Courts*. Santa Barbara, Calif.: Center for the Study of Democratic Institutions, 1960.

Rowan, Carl. *Dream Makers, Dream Breakers: The World of Justice Thurgood Marshall*. Boston: Little, Brown, and Co., 1993.

Tushnet, Mark. *Making Civil Rights Law: Thurgood Marshall and the Supreme Court, 1936–1961*. New York: Oxford University Press, 1994.

———. *Making Constitutional Law: Thurgood Marshall and the Supreme Court, 1961–1991*. New York: Oxford University Press, 1991.

Williams, Juan. *Thurgood Marshall: American Revolutionary*. New York: Time Books, Random House, 1998.

Mitchell, Clarence Maurice

"Clarence M. Mitchell: Civil Rights Lobbyist: New Spingarn Medalist." *Negro Heritage*, 8 (1969): 126–27.

"Clarence Mitchell: The Man on the Hill." *Crisis*, 87 (December 1980): 562.

"The Impact of Pure Brass: Clarence Mitchell, Jr." *Crisis*, 83 (April 1976): 122–26.

Pearson, Patricia A. "Clarence M. Mitchell, Jr. In *Notable Black American Men*, edited by Jessie Carney Smith. Detroit: Gale Research Inc., 1999, 822–23.

Watson, Denton L. *Lion in the Lobby: Clarence Mitchell, Jr.'s Struggle for the Passage of Civil Rights Laws*. New York: William Morrow & Co., 1990.

Williams, Michael W., ed. *The African American Encyclopedia*. North Bellmore, N.Y.: Marshall Cavendish, 1993.

Murphy, Carl John

Buni, Andrew. "Carl Murphy 1889–1967." In *Dictionary of American Negro Biography*, edited by Logan and Winston. New York: Norton & Co., 1982, 461–62.

Farrar, Hayward. *The Baltimore Afro-American, 1892–1950*. Westport, Conn.: Greenwood Press, 1998.

Good News For You! The Afro-American Newspapers. Baltimore: Afro-American Company, 1969.

Stoner, John C. "Carl Murphy." In *Contemporary Black Biography*, edited by Barbara Carlisle Bigelow. Vol. 4. Detroit: Gale Research Inc., 1994, 1882–83.

Murphy, John H., Sr. *Sergeant Murphy: The Story of a Civil War Veteran*. Baltimore: Baltimore Afro-American Company, 1942.

Murphy, Carl, William N. Jones, and William I. Gibson. "The *Afro*: Eastern Seaboard's Largest Weekly." *Crisis* (February 1938): 44–45, 50.

"This is Our War." [pamphlet, no author]. *Baltimore Afro-American*. Baltimore: Afro-American Company, 1942.

Wolseley, Roland E., Sr. *The Black Press, USA*. Ames: Iowa State University Press, 1990.

Murphy, John Henry, Sr.

Briscoe, Sherman. "John Henry Murphy Senior." In *Dictionary of American Negro Biography*, edited by Logan and Winston. New York: Norton & Co., 1982, 463.

Detweiler, Frederick G. *The Negro Press in the United States*. Chicago: University of Chicago Press, 1922, 1968.

Farrar, Hayward. *The Baltimore Afro-American, 1892–1950*. Westport, Conn.: Greenwood Press, 1998.

Penn, I. Garland. *The Afro-American Press and Its Editors*. Springfield, Mass.: Willey & Co., 1891.

Wolseley, Roland E., Sr. *The Black Press, USA*. Ames: Iowa State University Press, 1990.

Murray, Pauli

Diamonstein, Barbaralee. *Open Secrets: Ninety-four Women in Touch with Our Time*. New York: Viking Press, 1972.

Murray, Pauli. *Dark Testament and Other Poems*. Norwalk, Conn.: Silvermine Publishers, 1970.

———. *Proud Shoes: The Story of an American Family*. New York: Harper & Row, 1956.

———. *Song in a Weary Throat: An American Pilgrimage*. New York: Harper & Row, 1987.

Murray, Pauli and Leslie Rubin. *The Constitution and Government of Ghana*. London: Sweet & Maxwell, 1961.

Thomas, Gwendolyn. "Pauli Murray." *American Women Writers*. Vol. 125. New York: Frederick Tempar, 1981, 241–43.

Vick, Marsha C. "Pauli Murray." In *Notable Black American Women*, edited by Jessie Carney Smith. Detroit: Gale Research, Inc., 1999, 783–88.

Myers, Isaac

Bragg, George F. *Men of Maryland*. Baltimore: Church Advocate Press, 1914, 1925.

Foner, Philip S., and Ronald L. Lewis, eds. *The Black Worker: A Documented History from Colonial Times to the Present*. Vol. 1. Philadelphia: Temple University Press, 1978.

Jones, Robert L. "Isaac Myers." In *Notable Black American Men*, edited by Jessie Carney Smith. Detroit: Gale Research, Inc., 1998.

Matison, Summer E. "The Labor Movement and the Negro During Reconstruction." *Journal of Negro History*, 33 (1948): 426–68.

Thomas, Bettye C. "A Nineteenth Century Black Operated Ship Yard, 1866–1884: Reflection Upon Its Inception and Ownership." *Journal of Negro History*, 59 (1974): 1–12.

Pennington, James William Charles

Blackett, Richard. *Beating the Barriers: Biographical Essays in Nineteenth Century Afro-American History*. Baton Rouge: Louisiana State University Press, 1986.

———. *Building an Antislavery Wall: Black Americans in the Atlantic Abolition Movement, 1830–1860*. Baton Rouge: Louisiana State University Press, 1983.

Logan, Rayford. "James William Charles Pennington." In *Dictionary of American Negro Biography*, edited by Logan and Winston. New York: Norton & Co., 1982, 489–91.

Pennington, James. *The Fugitive Blacksmith: Or Events in the History of James W. C. Pennington, Pastor of a Presbyterian Church, New York, Former Slave in the State of Maryland, U.S.* London: Charles Gilpin, 1849.

———. *A Text Book of the Origin and History, Etc., Etc. of the Colored People*. Hartford: L. Skinner, 1841.

Quarles, Benjamin. *Black Abolitionists*. New York: Oxford University Press, 1970; New York: DaCapo Press, 1991.

Thomas, Herman E. *James W. C. Pennington: African American Churchman and Abolitionist*. New York: Garland Publishing, 1995.

Porter, James Amos

Driskell, David. *Hidden Heritage: Afro American Art, 1800–1950*. San Francisco, Calif.: The Association, 1985.

"*James A. Porter, Artist and Art Historian: The Memory of the Legacy.*" Washington, D.C.: Department of Art, Howard University, 1992.

Igoe, Lynn Moody. *Two Hundred Fifty Years of Afro-American Art: An Annotated Bibliography*. New York: R. R. Bowker Co., 1981.

Lewis, Samella S. *Art: African-Americans*. New York: Harcourt Brace Jovanovich, 1978.

Milton, Narissa Long. "James A. Porter." *Negro History Bulletin* (October 1954): 5–6.

Porter, James A. *Modern Negro Art*. New York: Arno Press, 1943.

Reynolds, Gary A., and Beryl J. Wright. *Against the Odds: African-American Artists and the Harmon Foundation*. Newark, N.J.: The Newark Museum, 1989.

Uzelac, Coni Porter. *James Amos Porter, 1905–1970: Spotlight on His Works on Paper*. Fort Lauderdale, Fla.: Westport Foundation and Gallery, 1998.

Yousef, Nancy and Renee Newman. "James Amos Porter." In *Encyclopedia of African-American Culture and History*, edited by Salzman, Smith, and West. New York: MacMillan Library Reference, 1996, 2188–89.

Quander, John Thomas

Cobb, William Montague. *Progress and Portents for the Negro in Medicine*. New York: National Association for the Advancement of Colored People, 1948.

Fauntroy, Walter E. "Tribute to the Quander Family." *U.S. Congressional Record*, April 10, 1984. Washington, D.C.: U.S. Government Printing Office, 1984, 1527.

Henderson, Rhonda. "Mount Vernon's Other Legacy," *Washington City Paper*. August 25, 1995, 9–10.

Qgwezi, Ben C. "Quander Family Boasts 300 Years of Black History," *The Washington Times*, February 22, 1990, B4–B5.

Quander, Rohulamin. "The History of the Quander Family." In *The Quanders United Tricentennial Celebration 1684–1984 Booklet*. Washington, D.C.: The Quanders United Incorporated, 1984, 27–45.

Still, Laurence A. "The Quanders: America's Oldest Black Family." *Ebony* (September 1984): 131, 133.

Thorton, Alvin, and Karen Williams. *Like a Phoenix I'll Rise: An Illustrated History of African Americans in Prince George's County, Maryland, 1696–1996*. Virginia Beach, Va.: The Donning Company, 1997, 103.

Quarles, Benjamin Arthur

Fisher, Vivian Njeri. "Benjamin A. Quarles." In *Notable Black American Men*, edited by Jessie Carney Smith. Detroit: Gale Research, Inc., 1999, 979–82.

Hembree, Michael. "Benjamin Quarles." In *Encyclopedia of African-American Culture and History*, edited by Salzman, Smith, and West. New York: MacMillan Library Reference, 1996, 2245–46.

Meier, August and Elliot Rudwick. *Black History and the Historical Profession, 1915–1980*. Urbana: University of Illinois Press, 1986.

Quarles, Benjamin, *Black Abolitionists*. New York: Oxford University Press, 1969.

———. *The Negro in the Making of America*. New York: Collier Books, MacMillan, 1987.

———. *The Negro in the Making of the American Revolution*. New York: Norton & Co., 1961.

Thorpe, Earl E. *Black Historians, A Critique*. New York: William Morrow, 1971.

Thomas, Vivien T.

Hamlett, Roz. "Cardiac Surgery's Invisible Man." *Johns Hopkins Magazine* (November 1993).

———. "Heart Surgery's Invisible Man." *Baltimore Sun*, November 4, 1993, 174.

Thomas, Vivien. *Partners of the Heart: Vivien Thomas and His Work with Alfred Blalock*. Philadelphia: University of Pennsylvania Press, 1985.

Tubman, Harriet Araminta Ross

Adler, David A. *Picture Book of Harriet Tubman*. New York: Holiday House, 1992. (Juvenile)

Bradford, Sarah H. *Harriet Tubman: The Moses of Her People*. New York: Corinth, 1961.

Clinton, Catherine. *Harriet Tubman: The Road to Freedom*. Boston: Little, Brown, 2004.

Conrad, Earl. *Harriet Tubman*. Washington, D.C.: The Associated Publishers, 1943.

Humez, Jean M. *Harriet Tubman: The Life and the Life Stories*. Madison: University of Wisconsin Press, 2003.

Larson, Kate Clifford. *Bound for the Promised Land: Harriet Tubman, Portrait of an American Hero*. New York: Ballantine, 2004.

Petry, Ann. *Harriet Tubman, Conductor on the Underground Railroad*. New York: Crowell, 1955. (Juvenile)

Quarles, Benjamin. "Harriet Tubman's Unlikely Leadership." In *Black Leaders of the Nineteenth Century*, edited by Leon F. Litwack and August Meier. Urbana: University of Illinois Press, 1988.

Ringgold, Faith. *Aunt Harriet's Underground Railroad in the Sky*. New York: Crown, 1992. (Juvenile)

Schroeder, Alan. *Minty: A Story of Young Harriet Tubman*. New York: Dial Books, 1996. (Juvenile)

Sterling, Dorothy. *Freedom Train: The Story of Harriet Tubman*. Garden City, N.Y.: Doubleday, 1961.

Taylor, M. W. *Harriet Tubman*. New York: Chelsea House, 1988.

Williams, Lorraine A. "Harriet Tubman." In *Dictionary of American Negro Biography*, edited by Logan and Winston. New York: Norton & Co., 1982.

Wallace, Phyllis Ann

Anderson, Bernard E. "Phyllis Ann Wallace." *American Economic Review*, 84 (1994): 91–92.

DeLongoria, Maria. "Phyllis Ann Wallace: A Black Woman Economist, and Public Policy." Master's thesis, Morgan State University, 1994.

Malveaux, Julianne. "Phyllis Ann Wallace: Economist, Educator, Scholar, Activist." In *Notable Black American Women*, edited by Jessie Carney Smith. Detroit: Gale Research, Inc., 1996, 1197–98.

———. "Tilting Against the Wind: Reflections in the Life and Work of Phyllis Ann Wallace." *American Economic Review* (May 1994): 93.

Rivlin, Alice. "Phyllis A. Wallace, Scholar and Activist." *Sloan Magazine* (Winter 1987): 19–22.

Walley, Augustus

Donaldson, Gary A. *The History of African Americans in the Military*. Malabar, Fla.: Krieger Publishing Company, 1991.

Downey, Fairfax D. *The Buffalo Soldiers in the Indian Wars*. New York: McGraw-Hill, 1969.

Leckie, William H. *The Buffalo Soldiers: A Narrative of the Negro Cavalry in the West*. Norman: University of Oklahoma Press, 1967.

Reef, Catherine. *Buffalo Soldiers*. New York: Twenty-first Century Books/Henry Holt & Company, Inc., 1993.

Schubert, Frank N. *Buffalo Soldiers, Braves and the Brass*. Shippensburg, Pa.: White Mane Publishing Co., 1993.

Sorokin, Ellen. "Buffalo Soldiers' Group Shares Black Cavalry's History." *The Washington Times*, February 14, 2000, C1, C2.

Wheeler, Major-General Joseph, et al. *Under Fire with the Tenth U.S. Cavalry: A Purely Military History of the Negro*. Chicago: American Publishing House, 1902.

Ward, Samuel Ringgold

Blackett, Richard. *Building an Antislavery Wall: Black Americans in the Atlantic Abolition Movement, 1830–1860*. Baton Rouge: Louisiana State University Press, 1983.

Burke, Ronald K. *Samuel R. Ward, Christian Abolitionist*. New York: Garland Publishers, 1995.

Ward, Samuel R. *Autobiography of a Fugitive Negro: His Anti-Slavery Labours in the United States, Canada and England*. New York: Arno Press, 1968.

Winks, Robin. "Samuel Ringgold Ward," *Dictionary of Canadian Biography*. Vol. 9. Toronto, Canada: University of Toronto Press, 1976.

Warner, Daniel Bashiel

Abingbade, Harrison O. "The Settler-African Conflicts: The Case of the Maryland Colonists and the Grebo, 1840–1900." *Journal of Negro History*, 66 (1980): 93–109.

Anderson, R. Earle. *Liberia: America's African Friend*. Chapel Hill: University of North Carolina Press, 1952.

Buell, Raymond Leslie. *Liberia: A Century of Survival, 1847–1947*. Africa Handbook, No. 7. Philadelphia: University of Pennsylvania Press, 1947.

Dolo, Emmanuel. *Democracy versus Dictatorship: The Quest for Freedom and Justice in Africa's Oldest Republic*. Lanham, Md.: University Press of America, 1996.

Huberich, Charles H. *The Political and Legislative History of Liberia*. Vol. I. New York: Central Book Co., 1947.

Moses, Wilson J. *Liberian Dreams: Back to Africa. Narratives from the 1850s*. University Park: Pennsylvania State University Press, 1998.

Richardson, Nathaniel R. *Liberia's Past and Present*. London: The Diplomatic Press & Publishing Co., 1959.

Shick, Tom W. *Behold the Promised Land: A History of Afro-American Settler Society in Nineteenth Century Liberia*. Baltimore: Johns Hopkins University Press, 1980.

Willey, Bell, ed. *Slaves No More: Letters from Liberia, 1833–1869*. Louisville: University of Kentucky Press, 1980.

Weems, Ann Maria

Carbone, Elisa. *Stealing Freedom*. New York: Alfred A. Knopf, 1998.

Cohen, Anthony. *The Underground Railroad in Montgomery County*. Rockville, Md.: Montgomery County Historical Society, 1994.

Harrold, Stanley. "Freeing the Weems Family: A New Look at the Underground Railroad." *Civil War History*, 42 (1996): 289–306.

Still, William. *The Underground Railroad: A Record*. Chicago: Johnson Publishing Company, Inc., 1872, 1970.

Welcome, Verda Freeman

Davis, Marianna W., ed. *Contributions of Black Women to America*. Vol. 2. Columbia, S.C.: Kenday Press, 1982.

Davis, Phillip. "Maryland Senator and Activist Verda Welcome is Dead." *Baltimore Sun*, April 24, 1990, 1A.

Hall, Wiley A., III. "Verda Welcome: Woman of Valor." *The Afro-American*, April 27, 1990, 1.

Nawrozki, Joe. "Verda Welcome Dies at 83, Renowned Maryland Lawmaker." *Baltimore Evening Sun*, April 23, 1990, A1, A7.

Newson, Moses J. "Mrs. Verda Welcome is First in Maryland History. *The Afro-American*, November 12, 1958, 1.

Page, Sterling. "The Lady Senator." *The Afro-American*, April 1, 1967.

Phillips, Glenn O. "Verda Freeman Welcome." In *Black Women in America: An Historical Encyclopedia*, edited by Darlene Clark Hine. Brooklyn: Carlson Publishing, Inc., 1993, 1241–42.

Radoff, Morris L., ed. *Maryland Manual 1863–1964*. Annapolis, Md.: Hall of Records Commission, 1964.

White, John. "Verda Welcome: The First Lady of Baltimore Politics." *Metropolitan*. Baltimore, Md., December 1979.

Young, N. Louise

Hathaway, Phyllis. "N. Louise Young, M.D." In *Notable Maryland Women*, edited by Winifred G. Helmes. Cambridge, Md.: Tidewater Publishers, 1977, 411–12.

Hilson, Robert, Jr. "Dr. N. Louise Young, 90." *Baltimore Sun*, September 25, 1997, 5B.

Sullivan, Jennifer. "Exhibit Traces History of Blacks in Medicine." *Baltimore Sun*, February 26, 1999, 3B.

"Young, N. Louise." *Who's Who Among Black Americans*. Farmington Hills, Minn.: The Gale Group, 1994, 1422.

Photo Credits

George "Father Divine" Baker, pp. 40–41
  Courtesy AP/World Wide Photos.

Benjamin Banneker, pp. 42–43
  Maryland Historical Society.

William Henry Bishop, pp. 44–45
  Courtesy Mrs. Joan Scurlock.

James Hubert "Eubie" Blake, pp. 46–47
  Courtesy Prints & Photographs Department, Moorland Springarn Research Center, Howard University.

George E. Bragg, pp. 48–49
  Courtesy Suzanne Chapelle.

John Edward Bruce, pp. 50–51
  Courtesy Photographs and Prints Division, Schomburg Center for Research in Black Culture, The New York Public Library, Astor, Lenox, and Tilden Foundations.

Cabell "Cab" Calloway, pp. 52–53
  Courtesy Prints & Photographs Department, Moorland Springarn Research Center, Howard University.

Albert Irvin Cassell, pp. 54–55
  Courtesy Prints & Photographs Department, Moorland Springarn Research Center, Howard University

Daniel Isaac Wright Coker, pp. 56–57
  Courtesy The Historical Society of Pennsylvania. Engraving of Daniel Coker, Sartain Collection.

Harry Augustus Cole, pp. 58–59
  Courtesy Morgan State University.

Silas Edwin Craft, pp. 60–61
  Courtesy Mrs. Dorothye Craft.

Harry Cummings, pp. 62–63
  Maryland Historical Society.

Ida Rebecca Cummings, pp. 64–65
  Maryland Historical Society.

Leon Day, pp. 66–67
  Courtesy National Baseball Hall of Fame Library, Cooperstown, New York.

Frederick Douglass, Cover and pp. 68–69
  "Samuel J. Miller, American, 19th Century, Frederick Douglass, daguerrotype, c. 1852. Photograph Courtesy of the Art Institute of Chicago.

Christian Abraham Fleetwood, pp. 70–71
  Courtesy Suzanne Chapelle.

E. Franklin Frazier, pp. 72–73
  Courtesy Prints & Photographs Department, Moorland Springarn Research Center, Howard University.

Joseph "Baby Joe" Gans, pp. 74–75
  Courtesy Theodore McKeldin Library, University of Maryland, College Park.

Henry Highland Garnet, pp. 76–77
  Courtesy Prints & Photographs Department, Moorland Springarn Research Center, Howard University.

Frances Ellen Watkins Harper, pp. 78–79
  Courtesy Prints & Photographs Department, Moorland Springarn Research Center, Howard University.

Josiah Henson, pp. 80–81
  Reproduction courtesy the Library of Congress.

Matthew Alexander Henson, pp. 82–83.
  Reproduction Courtesy the Library of Congress.

Billie Eleonora Holiday, pp. 84–85
  Courtesy Prints & Photographs Department, Moorland Springarn Research Center, Howard University.

Lillie Carroll Jackson, pp. 86–87
  Courtesy Suzanne Chapelle.

Mary Elizabeth Lange, pp. 88–89
  Courtesy the Sulpician Archives, Baltimore, Maryland.

Reginald Francis Lewis, pp. 90–91
  Courtesy Mrs. Loida Lewis.

Thurgood Marshall, pp. 92–93
  AP/Wide World Photos.

Clarence Maurice Mitchell, pp. 94–95
  Courtesy Prints & Photographs Department, Moorland Springarn Research Center, Howard University.

Carl John Murphy, pp. 96–97
  Courtesy Morgan State University.

John Henry Murphy, Sr., pp. 98–99
    Courtesy Maryland State Archives, MSA SC 2342-1-14.

Pauli Murray, pp. 100–101
    Courtesy the Schlesinger Library, Radcliffe College.

Isaac Myers, pp. 102–103
    Courtesy Suzanne Chapelle.

James W. Charles Pennington, pp. 104–105
    From Armistead, *A Tribute to the Negro,* opp. p. 408.
    Photocopy courtesy Library of Congress Photoduplica-
    tion Service.

James Amos Porter, pp. 106–107
    Courtesy Prints & Photographs Department, Moorland
    Springarn Research Center, Howard University.

John Thomas Quander, pp. 108–109
    Courtesy Mr. Rohulamin Quander.

Benjamin Arthur Quarles, pp. 110–111
    Courtesy Morgan State University.

Vivien Thomas, pp. 112–113
    Courtesy the Alan Mason Chesney Medical Archives of
    the Johns Hopkins Medical Institutions.

Harriet Araminta Ross Tubman, pp. 114–115
    Courtesy the Library of Congress.

Phyllis Ann Wallace, pp. 116–117
    Courtesy the MIT Museum.

Augustus Walley, pp. 118–119
    Courtesy Mrs. Betty Stokes.

Samuel Ringgold Ward, pp. 120–121
    Courtesy Prints & Photographs Department, Moorland
    Springarn Research Center, Howard University.

Daniel Bashiel Warner, pp. 122–123
    Courtesy the Historical Society of Pennsylvania. Portrait
    by Thomas Sully.

Ann Maria Weems, pp. 124–125
    Engraving from William Still, *The Underground Rail
    Road: A Record of Facts, Authentic Narratives, Letters,
    &c."* Philadelphia: Porter & Coates, 1872. Maryland
    Historical Society.

Verda Freeman Welcome, pp. 126–127
    Courtesy Maryland State Archives, MSA SC 1198.

N. Louise Young, pp. 128–129
    Maryland Historical Society.

Index

Bishop, William, 51
Bishop, William Henry, 23, **51, 137**
Bishop, William Henry, Sr., 14, 51
Black Enterprise, 123
blacksmiths, 6, 14, 111
Black Sox (Negro League), 29
"Black Tom," 9
"Black Yankee," 9
Blake, James Hubert "Eubie," 29, **53,**
  81, 137
Blalock, Alfred, 119
Blessed Peter Clavier School, 95
Blount, Clarence W., 40
Boegue, Rosine, 95
Boston Museum of Fine Arts, 123
Bowie State College, 21, 26, 27
boxing, 81
Boyne, Thomas, 125
Bragg, George Freeman, Jr., **55,** 105,
  137
Brett, Ruth, 117
bricklayers, 14
British-American Manual Labor
  Institute, 87
Broadus, Edward, 121
Brookings Institution, 123
Brooklyn Eagles, 73
Brown, Allen, and Watts, 65
Brown, John, 121
Brown, Tom, 10
Brown's Grove Beach, 30, 71
Brown v. Board of Education of Topeka,
  35, 99
Bruce, John Edward "Grit," **57**
Bruce, Martha, 57
Bruce, Robert, 57
Brune, John, 77
Buffalo Soldiers, 125
Bullock, Vera, 117
Bunche, Ralph, 99
Burey, Vivian "Buster," 99
Burns, Clarence "Du," 40
"Bury Me in a Free Land" (Harper), 85
buses, 107
Bush, George, 73
business owners, 14, 25
Butler, Benjamin F., 121
Butler, Lewis, 13
Butler, William, 23, 24
Butler, William, Jr., 24
Butts, Joseph Saifuss, 81
buyouts, 97
"Buy where you can work" campaign, 31

Caldwell, Gilbert, 135
Calloway, Blanche, 59
Calloway, Cabell (Cab), III, 29, **59,** 99
Calvert, Cecilius, 3
Cambridge, 24, 38, 69
Cambridge Orioles, 29
Campanella, Roy, 29
Canadian Antislavery Society, 127
Candle, John, 127
Carbone, Elisa, 131
Cargill, John Marcus, 23, 24, 69
Carnegie Hall, 91
Carney, Thomas, 9
carpenters, 6, 14
Carr, William T., 23
Carroll, Amanda Bowen, 93
Carroll, Charles, 93
Carter, James Earl "Jimmy," 101
carters, 14
Carver High School, 67
Cassell, Albert Irvin, **61**
Cassell, Charlotte, 61
Cassell, Gray and Sulton, 61
Catholics, 9, 16, 28, 95
Catonsville Social Giants, 29
caulkers, 14, 109
cavalrymen, 125
Cedar Hill, 75
Centenary Biblical Institute, 21
Center for Research on Women, 123
Chapin's Farm, battle of, 77
Chavis, Benjamin F., 97
Cheltenham School for Boys, 71
Chesapeake Marine Railway and Dry
  Dock Company, 109
Chestertown, 7
Christianity, 4, 15, 129
Church Advocate, 55
churches, 15. *See also specific churches by
  name*
Church of the Holy Nativity of
  Baltimore, 107
City Colored Band, 30
City Colored Orchestra, 30, 59
city councilmen, 24, 36, 40, 69
City Wide Young People's Forum, 31
Civil Rights Act of 1957, 101
Civil Rights Act of 1964, 38, 101
Civil Rights Movement, 37, 38, 93
Civil War, 18–19; battle of Chapin's
  Farm, 77; soldiers, 19, 75, 77, 83,
  125
Clark, Mary E. Hattie, 79

clergymen, 14, 25, 55, 63, 87, 107. *See
  also* preachers
Cleveland, Grover, 77
Coker, Daniel Isaac Wright, 12, 16, 17,
  63
Coker, Susan, 63
Cole, Emory, 36
Cole, Harry Augustus, 36, **65**
Cole, Richard Baker, 65
Cole, Rosina Thompson, 65
College Park, 36
colonial years, 3–7
Colored Building and Loan
  Association of Baltimore, 109
Colored Business Men's Association
  of Baltimore, 109
Colored Caulkers Trade Union Society
  of Baltimore, 109
Colored Citizen, 109
Colored Empty Stockings and Fresh
  Air Circle, 71
Colored High and Training School, 93
Colored High School Cadet Corps, 77
Colored Women's Suffrage Club, 135
Columbia, Md., 38
Commission on Interracial Problems
  and Relations, 34
Communists, 28
Conacher, Wenonah "Betty," 59
congressmen, 40
Conklin, Blanche, 69
Continental Congress, 9
Cook, Vivian Johnson, 25
cooks, 14
Cooksville Colored School, 67
Cooley, Denton, 119
Cooperative Womens' Civic League, 25
Coppin, Fannie Jackson, 22
Coppin State Normal School, 133
Coppin Teacher's College, 26
Corcoran Gallery of Art, 113
Coulbourne, William H. T., 23
Coulbourne and Jewett, 23
Craft, Ada Rebecca Graves, 67
Craft, Silas Birdsong, 67
Craft, Silas Edwin, **67**
craftsmen, 6, 14
Cummings, Elijah E., 40
Cummings, Eliza Jane Davage, 71
Cummings, Harry Sythe, 24, **69,** 71
Cummings, Henry, 69, 71
Cummings, Ida Rebecca, 25, 69, 71
Curry, Wayne, 40

housing, 22, 38, 69
Houston, Charles H., 93, 103
Howard, Martha, 105
Howard County, 38, 67
Howard County Center for African
American Culture, 67
Howard University, 61, 79, 107, 113,
125
Howard University Preparatory School,
115
Hughes, Langston, 93
Hunn, Ezekiel, 121

IBM, 113
immigrants, from rural areas, 27, 36
indentured servants, 3–4
Industrial Relations Research
Association, 123
International House, 113
"International Modest Code," 47
Iredell, Sara, 77

Jackson, James, 109
Jackson, Juanita, 31–32
Jackson, Kieffer, 93
Jackson, Lillie Carroll, 31, 93
Jamaica, 127
jazz, 53
Jefferson, Thomas, 49
Jenkins, Martin, 99
Jewett, Frederick S., 23
Jews, 9, 23, 28
job discrimination, 29
Johns Hopkins Hospital, 119
Johns Hopkins University, 22, 35, 37
Johnson, Annie, 125
Johnson, Anthony, 4
Johnson, Jack, 81
Johnson, John, 4
Johnson, John Wesley, 125
Johnson, Joshua, viii, 14
Johnson, Judy, 29
Johnson, Lyndon B., 38, 99, 111
Johnson, Mary, 4
Johnson, Richard, 4
Johnston, Emily, 53
Jones, Alvin "Mickey," 133
Jordan rebellion, 127
journalists, 57, 103
judges, 40, 41, 65, 99

Kennedy, John F., 99
Kensington Junior High School, 67

Francis Scott Key Junior High, 67
Kimbro, Henry, 29
kindergartens, 69, 71
Kindergarten Training School, 71
King, Hester, 25
King, Martin Luther, 38–39
Ku Klux Klan, 24, 28
Kunta Kinte, 5

labor unions, 109
Lady Sings the Blues (Holiday and
Dufty), 91
Lange, Annette, 95
Lange, Clovis, 95
Lange, Mary Elizabeth, 95
lawyers, 25, 65, 69, 97, 99, 107
Ledger, 55, 105
Levington, William, 16
Lewis, Lida M. Nicolas, 97
Lewis, Reginald Francis, 97
Liberia, 12, 77, 83, 105, 129
Liberty Party, 83, 127
Liberty ships, 33
Liberty Street Presbyterian Church, 83
libraries, 24
Library of Congress, 117
Lincoln, Abraham, 19, 83
Lincoln Athletic Club, 29
Lincoln University, 69, 77, 113
Lively, William, 17
lobbyists, 101
Lortt Ligonier, 5
Lundy, Benjamin, 11
Lyceum Observer, 77
lynchings, 28

Mahoney, George, 133
Maine Anti-Slavery Society, 85
Mandingo, 83
Manual Training School, 69
marriage: between blacks, 16; between
blacks and whites, 4; slave, 16
Marshall, Thurgood, 93, **99,** 103; and
Vivian "Buster" Burey, 99.
Maryland, 3–43; antebellum period,
12–18; Civil War experience, 18–
19; colonial years, 3–7; early
abolitionism in, 10–12; early
twentieth century, 24–34;
Reconstruction in, 19–23;
Revolutionary period, 8–10. *See
also specific cities by name*
Maryland Athletic Hall of Fame, 81

Maryland Bar Association, 65
Maryland Colonization Society, 12, 77
Maryland Colored State Industrial Fair
Association, 109
Maryland Commission on Negro
History and Culture, 117
Maryland Committee for Passage of
Abortion Laws, 135
Maryland Committee to Prevent
Passage of Voluntary Sterilization
laws, 135
Maryland Constitution of 1776, 9
Maryland Constitution of 1864, 19
Maryland Constitution of 1867, 20–
21
Maryland Council of Defense, 135
Maryland Court of Appeals, 41, 65
Maryland Elks, 71, 135
Maryland Gazette, 10
Maryland Home, 55
Maryland Home for Friendless
Colored Children, 55
Maryland House of Delegates, 10, 36,
40, 65
Maryland in Liberia, 12
Maryland Masons, 109
Maryland National Guard, 28
Maryland Society for Promoting the
Abolition of Slavery and the Relief
of Poor Negroes and Others
Unlawfully Held in Bondage, 11
Maryland State Advisory Commission
to the United States Civil Rights
Commission, 38
Maryland State Senate, 65, 133
Maryland State Treasurer, 41
Maryland Training School, 135
Maryland Women's Hall of Fame, 93
Masonic organizations, 16, 109
Massachusetts Anti-Slavery Society, 75
May, Samuel J., 121
mayors, 40
McCall Pattern Company, 97
McCulloh Planned Parenthood Clinic,
135
McGuinn, Warner T., 24
McHenry, James, 49
McKeldin, Theodore, 34, 65, 93, 135
McKenny, John, 87
McKnight, Dorothye Beatryce, 67
McPherson, Josiah, 87
Medal of Freedom, 53, 101
Medal of Honor, 19, 77, 125

Taussig, Helen, 119
teachers, 13, 25, 71, 103, 133
term slaves, 13
theaters, 29
Thomas, A. Jack, 30
Thomas, Vivien T., 119
Thompson, Thomas Arrington, 24
Thompson, William H., 23
Tilghman, Frisby, 111
Tilghman, James, 111
TLC Group Company, 97
tobacco, 5, 6
Toronto Maple Leafs, 73
trains, 22–23, 111
Truman, Albert, 61
Truman, Harry, 34, 53
Trunkett, Ralph, 4
Tubman, Harriet (Araminta) Ross,
    11–12, 19, 121
Tubman, John, 121
Harriet Tubman High School, 67
Harriet Tubman House for Indigent
    and Aged Negroes, 121
Turner, Nat, 11
Tuskegee Airmen, 33, 67
Tuskegee Institute, 61
Tyler, Marion Grant, 53

"Uncle Tom," 87
Uncle Tom's Cabin (Stowe), 87
Underground Railroad, 11, 83, 85, 87,
    121, 131
Union Army, 19
Union Memorial Hospital, 65, 135
Union Missionary Society, 111
Union Navy, 19
Union Seminary, 17, 85
United Nations Educational Scientific
    and Cultural Organization
    (UNESCO), 79
University of Maryland, 22, 26, 35–
    36; desegregation of, 93; Graduate
    School, 35; Law Department, 69;
    School of Law, 26, 65, 99; School
    of Nursing, 35
U.S. Army: 9th and 10th Cavalry
    Regiments, 125
U.S. Colored Troops: 30th Regiment,
    105
U.S. Colored Volunteer Infantry: 4th
    Regiment, 77
U.S. Commission for Racial Justice, 97

U.S. Constitution: 22; Nineteenth
    Amendment 25, 99
U.S. Department of Labor, 123
U.S. House of Representatives, 40
U.S. Supreme Court, 99
Uzelac, Constance Burnett Porter, 113

Valiant Women's Democratic Club of
    Baltimore, 133
Van Buren, Martin, 127
Victoria, Queen, 87, 121
Vietnam War, 38
vote, right to, 22
voter registration, 93
Voting Rights Act of 1965, 38, 101
Vox Africanorum, 10

Wallace, Phyllis Ann, **123**
Walley, Augustus, **125**
Ward, Samuel Ringgold, 127
Warner, Daniel Bashiel, 12, **129**
Warner, Jacob, 129
War on Poverty, 38
Washington, Booker T., 55, 69, 105
Washington, George, 115
Washington Cadet Corps, 77
Washington Evening Star, 113
Booker T. Washington Junior High
    School, 123
Waters, Ethel, 29
Watkins, Levi, 119
Watkins, William, 17, 85
Watkins' Academy, 85
Watty, Hiram, 69
wealth, 97
Webb, Chick, 29
Weems, Addison, 131
Weems, Ana Maria, **131**
Weems, Arabella, 131
Weems, Augustus, 131
Weems, Catherine, 131
Weems, John, 131
Weems, John Junior, 131
Weems, Joseph, 131
Weems, Tom, 131
Welcome, Henry C., 133
Welcome, Verda Freeman, 36, **133**
Wells, Lewis, 14
Welsh, Molly, 4, 49
West Africa, 63, 77
West Baltimore, 69
Westerfield Award, 123

Whatcoat Methodist Episcopal
    Church, 81
Phyllis Wheatley Elementary School, 123
Wheeler, Joseph, 125
White, Andrew, 3
Whyte, Violet Hill, 31
Williams, Anita Rose, 25
Wilson, Jud, 29
Wilson, Ted, 91
Wilson, W. Llewellyn, 30, 53, 59
Wilson, William, 125
women, 9; Civil War experience of, 19;
    early twentieth century, 25–26
Women's Christian Temperance
    Union, 85
women's organizations, 25
Women's Republican League, 71
Women's Rights Convention, 75
Works Progress Administration
    (WPA), 32, 107
World Anti-Slavery Convention
    (1843), 111
World Peace Society, 111
World War I, 27, 69, 125
World War II, 32–33, 73
WPA. *See* Works Progress
    Administration
Wright, Edward, 63
Wright, Isaac, 63
Wright, Joe, 131
writers, 57, 103
Wynn, Albert R., 40

Yokely, Laymon, 73
Young, Alfred, 135
Young, Estelle, 135
Young, Howard, 135
Young, N. Louise, **135**
Young Democrats, 133
Young Men's Christian Association
    (YMCA), 30
Young People's Forum. *See* City Wide
    Young People's Forum
Young's Pharmacy, 135
Young Women's Christian Association
    (YWCA), 71, 93
Youth Unemployment Projects, 101